The Way to True Peace and Rest

The Way to True Peace and Rest

Six Sermons on Hezekiah's Sickness
Isaiah 38:1-22

Robert Bruce

*Translated and Edited by
David C. Searle*

THE BANNER OF TRUTH TRUST

THE BANNER OF TRUTH TRUST
3 Murrayfield Road, Edinburgh, EH12 6EL, U.K.
P.O. Box 621, Carlisle, PA 17013, U.S.A.

*

First published in
Sermons by the Rev. Robert Bruce, Minister of Edinburgh. Edited by
Rev. William Cunningham (Edinburgh: Wodrow Society, 1843)

This edition translated and edited by David C. Searle, 2017

*

ISBN
Print: 978 1 84871 749 7
EPUB: 978 1 84871 750 3
Kindle: 978 1 84871 751 0

*

Typeset in Adobe Garamond Pro 10.5/13.5 pt at
The Banner of Truth Trust, Edinburgh

Printed in the U.S.A. by
Versa Press, Inc.,
East Peoria, IL

For my twin brother John
with gratitude for the grace and love of God
exhibited in our lives and in our relationship together
over the past eighty years

Contents

Sermon 3: Isaiah 38:7-11

Sermon 4: Isaiah 38:12-14

Introduction

E VER since I ministered in Larbert Kirk for ten years
(1975–85), where from 1625 to 1631 Robert Bruce preached
in the original church, the remains of which are still to be
seen in the adjacent graveyard, I have been fascinated and
challenged by this great man's life and ministry. He was born
(c. 1554) in nearby Airth Castle, now a prestigious hotel. His
father, Sir Alexander Bruce endowed Robert, his second son,
with the barony of Kinnaird and built for him a large country
seat; although Kinnaird House has been rebuilt, behind it still
stands the original stabling which Master Robert would have
used as a young man.

His father anticipated that he would become a senator
in the College of Justice, and so he studied law in St
Andrews, France, and Louvain. But Robert Bruce turned
his back on earthly prestige and decided to enter the ministry of the Kirk of Scotland. However, his mother, Janet
Livingstone, a great-granddaughter of James I, was a
devout Roman Catholic, and opposing such a vocation
she insisted that he renounce his right to barony with

its substantial income and lands before he returned to St Andrews to study for the ministry. There Andrew Melville became a significant influence on him.

In 1587 the General Assembly voted for him to become minister of St Giles' in Edinburgh and the very next year he was elected as Moderator of the Assembly, a clear indication of the extraordinary high regard in which he was already held throughout the Kirk. For a time he was a favourite of James VI who appointed him a Privy Councillor in 1589; the following year he anointed Anne of Denmark at her coronation as James' Queen.

After the murder of the Earl of Gowrie in 1600, when Bruce refused to declare from the pulpit of St Giles' the king's version of the assassination, James banished him to France, then to Inverness (1605–13), then to confinement at Kinnaird (1613–22), and finally back to Inverness until James' death in 1625. Charles I was persuaded to permit him to return to Kinnaird, where he lived from 1625 until his death in 1631. During those final six years of his life, he preached regularly in Larbert Kirk, and many from far and near flocked to sit under his ministry, some of whom became significant figures in the ongoing life of the Kirk.

Through Bruce's influence it is widely acknowledged that in spite of his years of banishment he was instrumental in bringing the Scottish Church into a period of greater maturity and stability. His mortal remains were buried beneath the pulpit in the Kirk at Larbert. During my time at Larbert, and with the kind permission of Lord Elgin, his kinsman, I arranged for the burial headstone to be brought into the vestibule of the present church building, in order to preserve it from further erosion. Incidentally, Lord Elgin still has in his possession Bruce's copy of the Geneva Bible (often called 'The Breeches Bible').

I have found no record of the date of the six sermons on Isaiah 38 preached in St Giles', the first two in the presence of James VI, but because of the reference in the third sermon to the recent defeat of the Spanish Armada, they were probably preached some time in the period 1588–90.

Regarding the task of preparing these sermons for publication, I can do no better than to quote from Professor T. F. Torrance's explanation in his Introduction to *The Mystery of the Lord's Supper* which was published in 1957.[1]

> Scholars will want to turn to the original text. This edition is not for them but for the general membership of the Kirk, the successors of those to whom the sermons were first delivered. While trying to keep as close as possible to the original text, and to preserve Bruce's striking style, I have taken the liberty of arranging clauses and sentences again and again in order to bring out more clearly the logic of the argument, and frequently also of shortening them when the exposition seemed needlessly repetitious, at least according to modern standards.

Unlike Professor Torrance, in footnotes I have cited many of the Scripture quotations as in the Geneva Bible (indicated as 'GenB'). I have done this because at times Bruce's interpretation does depend on the rendering of the translation he used. Several times in the earlier chapters I have also suggested

---

[1] With Professor Torrance's permission, republished by Christian Focus Publications (Fearn, Ross-shire), in 2005.

in footnotes where it seemed to me highly probable that Bruce was using Calvin's *Commentary on Isaiah*. It would make an interesting study to follow this through in much more detail, but I often became aware that frequently—though by no means always—Bruce's understanding and insights into the text had almost certainly been stimulated by Calvin's exposition of the same passage. I thought that a few examples of such similarities of interpretation between Bruce and the great reformer would be of interest to some readers.

With the kind permission of the Very Revd Professor I. R. Torrance who holds his father's copyright, I have included as an Appendix the first part of Bruce's fourth sermon on the Lord's Supper. I have done this to help readers to understand Bruce's persistent insistence that his hearers keep guard on a cleansed conscience; it is a most important and dominant theme in his preaching. Calvin has this same emphasis in his sermons and Bible studies. Bruce's contemporary, the Cambridge theologian and Puritan, William Perkins (1558–1602), also wrote extensively on conscience as well as on the frame of mind in which the Lord's supper should be taken.[2] I have taken the liberty of adding to this volume an additional 'one-off' sermon which I translated some years ago: 'An Exhortation to the Presbyteries of Lothian'; it is full of sound biblical sense and gives a further insight into our forefathers' theological and practical faithfulness to the reformed faith.

---

[2] William Perkins, *A case of conscience: the greatest that euer was; how a man may know whether he be the child of God or no. Resolued by the word of God.* (1592); *The foundation of Christian religion: gathered into sixe principles. And it is to bee learned of ignorant people, that they may be fit to hear sermons with profit, and to receiue the Lords Supper with comfort* (1591).

Finally, I am grateful to those friends who kindly checked the sermon scripts for typos: Ian Barter, Frances McLeod, Alistair Simpson and Dr Sandy Waugh. My gratitude also to the staff of the Banner of Truth Trust, for their courteous helpfulness at all times.

David C. Searle

Stonefall Lodge
Grange, Perthshire
January, 2017

The First Sermon

Upon the 38th Chapter of the Prophecy of Isaiah

Preached in the Presence of the King's Majesty

In those days Hezekiah became sick and was at the point of death. And Isaiah the prophet the son of Amoz came to him, and said to him, 'Thus says the LORD: Set your house in order, for you shall die, you shall not recover.' ² Then Hezekiah turned his face to the wall and prayed to the LORD, ³ and said, 'Please, O LORD, remember how I have walked before you in faithfulness and with a whole heart, and have done what is good in your sight.' And Hezekiah wept bitterly.—Isaiah 38:1-3

IN the words that I have just read, beloved in Christ Jesus, the serious disease into which this godly king fell is now described, and the way he reacted during his illness is clearly set down. It pleased the Lord to exercise this godly king with this grievous trial, amongst many others; and though it is true various sicknesses are common to all humanity, yet our reaction and how we behave when struck with such an illness are by no means common. Therefore, let us take heed to the various aspects of this account, that we may learn how to conduct ourselves in the event of our suffering some serious disease; thus, learning from king Hezekiah's behaviour, we may come to obtain the same comfort he experienced.

At the beginning of this chapter, the king is afflicted by a grievous illness, the symptoms and effects of which are not revealed, apart from what may be gathered from verse 21, to which I shall firstly draw your attention. Second, the time when he fell ill is noted. Third, the gravity and pain of his illness are also noted. Finally, the way in which the king reacted under such a serious affliction is set down for us.

The nature of the disease

Firstly, we learn from verse 21 that the nature of the disease was an extremely painful boil, for the same [Hebrew] word is used here as we find in Exodus 9:9, a purulent kind of boil that has a number of heads and pustules, according to the actual meaning of the word. In the days of Pharaoh it was a very deadly pestilence. Indeed, since then, as the world has grown in wickedness there has been produced various kinds of visitations[1] not previously known; here in our own city we have experience of the same divine afflictions. For as men are ingenious in inventing new sins to provoke God to wrath, the Lord being both just and wise responds with new visitations and plagues to punish these new sins. For the storehouse of the Lord's judgment can never be emptied.

However, surely it is surprising that God should have visited so godly a king with so terrible a plague, since this kind

[1] The Scots word used is 'botches' which meant 'visitations sent by God as serious or potentially fatal illnesses'.

of affliction normally proceeds from his hot rage and wrath. For the divine anger is expressed in Scripture in various ways such as 'the finger of the Lord', or 'the dread by night', or 'the arrow that flies by day', or 'a devouring plague'. Thus, as I say, it is most surprising that a king who was so greatly loved by God should have been afflicted by him so publicly before the whole world. What then are we to learn from this?

This visitation upon the king teaches us two necessary lessons.

First, it teaches us not to measure the favour or displeasure of God by any external event here on earth. For if we consider some visitation of God upon his child, if we dwell on the nature of the plague or affliction, both its quality and quantity, if we look to the lengthy duration of the plague, in the opinion of onlookers and of the person who is afflicted, after some time he will begin to think he is in a worse case than any of the reprobate. But however it may be regarded in the heart and judgment of man, it is far otherwise in the judgment and heart of God. For hidden in the heart of God concerning those who are his children is one purpose, but a very different purpose concerning the reprobate. I will explain: when the affliction is common to us and to them, the cause for the affliction is by no means the same, neither is God's purpose the same. As to the godly, our affliction flows from the favour, love and mercy of God in Christ Jesus and is directed towards our great profit and advantage, that is, that we being corrected here may not perish in eternity along with the wicked of this world.

On the other hand, the affliction visited on the reprobate flows from the burning wrath and indignation of God, as from the righteous Judge; for he is initiating the punishment in this life that will continue for all eternity. Therefore, as affliction to the ungodly is the harbinger of divine judgment, for those who love him it is a merciful correction.

In Isaiah chapter 27 the prophet expresses this matter so vividly that I think there is no part of Scripture in which there is greater comfort. In verses 4, 7[2] he says to the kirk, 'I am not', says he, 'in fury, I am not in a rage, supposing I strike you; indeed, suppose I strike you', says he, 'I do not strike you as I strike those who strike you. I do not slay you as I slay those who slay you; for in striking you I purge you from your iniquity, in striking you I remove your sins from you; but I do not so with the rest.'

The first lesson, therefore, that you have to learn here is this: do not measure the favour of God by any external event here on earth, whether it be prosperity or adversity.

The second thing you have to learn here is this: you see that kings may suffer from a divinely visited affliction. There is no prince on earth exempted from the judgments of God, when it pleases him to administer them. So much then for the nature of Hezekiah's disease.

The timing of this disease

Secondly, we are told the time when the king fell ill. Although there is not specific time given in my text, we are told that it

---

[2] Isa. 27:4, 7: 'Angre is not in me: who wolde set the briers and the thornes against me in battel? I wolde go through them, I wolde burne them together. … Hathe he smitten him as he smote those that smote him? or is he slayne according to the slaughter of them that were slane by him' (Geneva Bible, 1560).

was after the king of Assyria took up arms against Hezekiah. Therefore it was in the fourteenth year of his reign that he became ill; for this godly king reigned twenty-nine years, fifteen of them were given to him after his illness. In the fourteenth year of his reign the wars began, and this time of sickness relates to those events. Whether the disease was after the siege or during it the opinion of the scholars varies. But in 2 Chronicles 32 it appears that he fell ill after the siege and the deliverance from it,[3] for we read there that when the invader approached Jerusalem, Hezekiah began to repair the defensive city walls and stopped up the conduits [to deny water to the Assyrians]. He sent messages to Isaiah and he went to the temple to pray. This all seems to indicate that the king was fit and well; there is nothing to suggest he was a sick man. So it appears that it was after the siege that he fell ill.

Now pay close attention to where my reasoning is leading. The king is scarcely freed when he falls into a serious illness. And so we perceive that a man of royal status, a most godly and excellent prince, is subject to continual troubles and vexation, so that the outcome of one trial is the beginning of but another. So it pleased the Lord to order them. And to what end, I pray you? To the end that this life, with all its pleasures and glories, may become bitter to the taste and so that he may be moved to look for a better life.

This lesson pertains to all Christians. For if you are a Christian, expect trouble, O man! There is no other way than for you daily to take up your cross and follow Christ. As for the 'fatted-calves'[4] of this world, the Lord in his righteous

---

[3] See 2 Chron. 32:20-26.
[4] Bruce's phrase is 'fed-marts'.

judgment has appointed them for slaughter. But if you are someone not appointed by God for slaughter, yet are subject to some continual divine discipline, either in soul or in body, in family or in reputation, one way or other be submissive to God's correction. There is no other way to pierce the clouds except through some ongoing trial.

Since this is so it becomes us not to have our hearts grunting[5] here on earth but it becomes us to have our hearts at ease, and our minds lifted up to the heavens where our Master reigns in glory, and to use the things of this world as they may best prepare us for the next world; otherwise, terrible will be the judgment and shame that the things of this world will bring upon us. So much, then, for the timing of Hezekiah's disease.

The gravity and pain of this illness

Third, in the verses that I have read the gravity of the illness is made clear in several ways. First Isaiah tells us that the king 'became sick and was at the point of death'.[6] Second, the gravity of the illness is confirmed when Isaiah is commanded by God to tell him that he will die and not recover. Third, the boil that struck him was deadly, making clear the seriousness of his illness.

In the king's extremity the prophet visited him and enjoined him to do two things. The first was to set his house in order. The second was to prepare himself for death, and in

---

[5] Bruce's original word is the braid Scots 'gruntling' used of 'ane troup of porcks with hiddius din, grewous gruntling…'. He is continuing the metaphor of the abattoir begun with the 'fed-marts', i.e., 'fatted-calves'.

[6] 'About that time was Hezekiah sicke vnto the death', verse 1a (GenB).

order to draw his heart away from material things and earthly comforts, he assured him that he was about to die. Indeed, he reinforced his words by adding that he would not recover.[7] It is such a hard thing to get the hearts of kings dragged away from their wealth and glory.

The prophet's visit to the king teaches us something of our duty towards those of our [Christian] brothers who are experiencing the same kind of divine visitation. In these circumstances we must be humane, loving and righteous, and that applies especially to those to whom has been entrusted the care of souls and whose office represents the close-knit bonds of affection.[8] At such times we pastors are bound to call on our brethren for it is then that the devil is most busy, so that the brother's physical condition distracts him from hearing God's word and former sins begin to revive and haunt his memory. It is then that there is great need of comfort.

We are also taught here by the prophet how to present our comfort, lest we spend out time in idle and unprofitable conversation, as do worldly people. First then, we should advise the sick person to set his affairs in order, and write his will and thus turn his thoughts from material things, so that his heart may be ready to leave this world when the Lord calls him home. But the vast majority of people neglect to prepare themselves for the end of life which is why so few

[7] 'Thus saith the Lord, Put thine house in an ordre, for thou shalt dye, and not liue', verse 1b (GenB).

[8] Bruce's phrase is 'who represent Esay in our office'. 'Esay' is a Scots' word with about a dozen quite different and apparently unrelated connotations; the ninth definition in DSL seems the right one here: 'used of a joining-together, friendship, bonds or ties of affection: tight-knit, close, intimate.'

are ready to depart when the Lord summons them; then they are compelled to leave behind things they would fain cling to and those possessions on which they have set their affections, because they have regarded this world and their homes here as their permanent dwelling-place.

The truth is that during their life-time they have not so much as thought about the day they will die, but always they have told they are bound to live for many years to come. And what amazes me most is that there is hardly a single person who warns them to prepare for the inevitable, not even when the Lord himself begins to lay his hand upon them through some terminal illness. Some say, 'We don't want to upset them and make their illness worse.' Others visit them and say, 'We should tell them how serious their sickness is, but it will only upset us to do so.' Even their doctor says to them, 'Your constitution is still strong, so don't worry!' Therefore, if their pastor neglects his duty to speak plainly to them, there is hardly a friend who will warn them to prepare themselves before their mental faculties begin to fail.

Since then it is the minister's bounden duty to propose that the sick person set his house in order, it is that man's duty to act on his counsel. For this warning is coming from God himself, and not merely from the minister who in brotherly affection[9] passes it on from the Lord. Such pastoral care is not only for kings, but is for all heads of families to whom God has given the responsibility for their households, not only during their lifetime, but also immediately prior to their death. In this way disagreements and disputes are to be avoided after the family's head has died. In the Scriptures, both the

[9] See Note 8 above on 'Esay'.

patriarchs and godly kings have left us an example concerning this, therefore I will not press the point any further.

Once all material affairs have been dealt with, and a man's conscience is at peace, his soul is now ready to hear about his impending death. And so the prophet comes, as we have noted, to confirm the gravity of the illness. Indeed, dear friends, in Isaiah's announcement it is clear he is very direct. That directness arose from the divine commission given to him, 'Thus saith the Lord, "Put your house in order, for you shall die and not live."' Today, however, we do not have such a plain warrant, therefore we may not be so direct with the sick person. Nevertheless, we ought always to exhort him to examine his conscience, to unburden his soul and to make himself ready, for whenever it shall please the Lord to call. In short, the main purpose of the pastoral visit hangs on these two points: first, to bid the sick person to turn aside from the things of this world; second, to exhort him to prepare for the world to come.

The first seeming error in Isaiah's message

However, before I leave the prophet's pronouncement, there would seem to be within it three errors.

1 First, it appears that the prophet's pronouncement is over-severe against such a godly king and treats him too harshly when he was an ill man; for Isaiah begins his message by taking from him all hope of recovery. He acts very differently to the usual doctor, for if they consider some illness to be terminal they do not tell that to the patient, but only to a few of his friends. By contrast, the prophet announces to the king his imminent demise. It would have seemed callous if it had been spoken to some pagan who has neither knowledge of God nor hope of heaven and therefore thinks that there is nothing beyond death. Similarly, the prophet's words would have appeared insensitive even to a completely godless man, which leads me to the prophet's next apparent error.

Further, as Solomon warns, 'Oh! how bitter is the death of those who live according to the flesh.'[10] Yet, even to those who live carnal, godless lives, Isaiah's message would have seemed hard and extreme. I ask you, why should death be so bitter to them? The reason is that in the anguish of death they become aware of the separation of the soul from the body. In addition, they are also aware of their sin gnawing at them and of the impending wrath of God burning against their wickedness. This sense of the divine anger strikes horror into their soul, so that they tremble at the very thought of death. Therefore I say that the prophet's message to such persons would have been like cruel threatening.

But for Christians and for a godly king as was Hezekiah, Isaiah's words were not so harsh. For we who believe must not regard death as unbelievers do, but we must think of death as she has now become in the goodness and mercy of God in Christ Jesus. For Christians, is not death robbed of her sting? Is she not sanctified to us in the death of Christ? And has she not been transformed for us into the entrance to perpetual

---

[10] Bruce may be alluding to several proverbs: 'fooles shall dye for want of wisdome. The blessing of the Lord, it maketh riche, and he doeth adde no sorowes with it. It is as a passe time to a foole to do wickedly: ... That which the wicked feareth, shall come vpon him: ... As the whirle winde passeth, so is the wicked no more...' (Prov. 10:21-25; GenB).

happiness? Is she not the way back from our banishment and our passage into the eternal heavens? Therefore, looking upon death not as the end of mortal living, but as she has been made unto us in Christ, at the sound of her call we ought to lift up our eyes, and rejoice that the redemption of our souls is near. And when that final time of departure comes and the Lord summons us, we ought also to rejoice, since he had made death for us but a step to joy, and a harbinger of loving reunions.

But it is not possible that mere words can induce men to prepare themselves for death. The most effective way to avoid the horror of death is to think upon death. Yet, notwithstanding the various awesome events we witness daily, not a single hair on our heads is moved! The only and most obvious means to prepare ourselves for death, as I have already said, is to start to live here and now the kind of life that we are meant to live. You man, change the direction of your living; you man, conform your life here with that life to come, and when there is complete harmony between your earthly and heavenly life, death will be to you the entrance to that everlasting joy. You man, bid all your foul affections farewell, for both you and they cannot enter heaven. You man, bid goodnight to the sin to which you are a slave and a lowly servant; for unless your ways are altered, you man, do not think that death shall be a pathway to eternal life. Therefore learn, all of you who long for a pleasant death, so to rule and order this earthly life that it may agree in some measure with the life to come.

The second seeming error in Isaiah's message

The second 'speck in the eye' in the prophet's announcement is that it appears to be superfluous. Why? From the nature of his illness his death seemed certain, so his physicians will have told him, and so the weakness of his sick body would have already indicated. But Isaiah's words were by no means superfluous when we think about our human natures and how loath all of us are to die. For we know by experience that there are some who will scarcely admit they are dying, even right up to their very last gasp.

The love we have for this life is known to us all. That was why the prophet so directly announced death to him so that in this way the king might be moved to raise his hope above earthly things and all human help and to seek the support, denied to him by nature, from God alone. Thus, far from being superfluous, the prophet's words were the most effective means to bring him to order his steps aright.

The third seeming error in Isaiah's message

The final 'speck in the eye' is that the Lord appears in the prophet's words to dissemble. For is this not blatant dissimulation to tell him that he will die, yet to mean the opposite?[11] So it appears that God is only pretending in his prophet's message that the king was about to die, when his actual purpose for him was that he should live a further fifteen years! To answer this charge the principle must be laid down that attached to all God's warnings and promises there is always a

---

[11] As in verse 5: 'Go, & say vnto Hezekiah, Thus saith the Lord God of David thy father, I haue heard thy praier, & sene thy teares: behold, I wil adde vnto thy daies fiftene yeres' (GenB).

condition; the condition is either secretly enclosed or is later made clear. Scripture gives us evidence of this as in Ezekiel 18 and Daniel 4:27.[12]

This then being the nature of God's ominous warnings, Isaiah's terrible words, for terrible they appeared to be, nevertheless they contained within them a condition: namely, the king would die unless he turned to the Lord, sought his face and had recourse to prayer. It was the same as with Nineveh: the Lord fully intended to punish the city unless they stayed his hand by their repentance. So I repeat, all God's promises and threatenings have a condition attached, which is either explicitly stated or secretly implied. Therefore the king lived because those terrible words contained a secret condition. The directness of the message was not intended to drive him to despair, but rather to bring him urgently to seek grace and recovery at the hands of the living God.

Now that I have touched upon the seriousness, the occasion and nature of the king's illness, let us learn the usefulness of this; for it is necessary that this doctrine be applied to our generation.

The state of our nation

We give thanks to God that our own king is not struck down with some illness. But surely his realm is seriously sick. For as long as Popery remains among us along with their pestilent

---

[12] 'Haue I anie desire that the wicked shulde dye, saith the Lord God? or shal he not liue, if he returne from his waies?' (Ezek. 18:23; GenB). [Then Daniel said] 'Wherefore, o King, let my counsel be acceptable vnto thee, and break of thy sinnes by righteousnes, & thine iniquities by mercie toward the poore: lo, let there be an healing of thine errour.' (Dan. 4:27; GenB).

leaders, and as long as floods of iniquity continue to flow from many of our great men, heavy judgment hangs over our land. In all conscience, I cannot but expect heavy judgment until these sins be removed. There is hardly a great man who does not think that he can please himself in any way he chooses. Not only here in this city but in other parts of our nation gross sins are committed and the kirk is taken advantage of by everyone. There is disdain and contempt for the word from the greatest to the least. Unless these things be purged away, I can only expect the Lord to raise up some—even from the furthest Indies—to plague this land.

I have no doubt that judgment has been delayed on account of the tears and sighs of the godly as well as the fact that the kirk is now free from its former bondage. Indeed, I am certain of this, and therefore I pray that God may so work in your heart, your majesty, by his grace that you may put your hand to purge your part of these islands. The Lord in his mercy establish your heart by his grace that, however some may seek to influence you, you will refuse to take part in other men's sins.

There are three ways in which we may share responsibility for others' sins: first, when in both thought and action we share some sin with them; [second,] when we consent but only in our hearts; third, when we turn a blind eye instead of reproving, and tolerate when we should punish. It is in the third way that magistrates tend to be guilty. So much for the application.

We think now about my text in Isaiah 38.

The king's behaviour in his sickness

We must now consider the way the king reacted when he was smitten with so terrible an illness; we find this clearly recorded in verses 2 and 3. I cannot add to this subject any more than the text tells us. I do not deny that Hezekiah may have said much more to Isaiah than is recorded, but what does the Scripture tell us? We learn that he sought to be alone so that he could turn to God in prayer. We know that he prayed from the heart, for we also learn that he wept bitterly. Such sorrow surely is evidence that his prayer flowed from his heart and was offered in the right spirit. For if God was to leave us on our own we would not know either what to say in prayer or even how to pray. But, as we read in Romans 8:26, it is the Spirit of God who directs our prayers that issue in great sighs and tears, and who causes our hearts to melt as with Hezekiah. So it is clear from the earnestness of his praying that it flowed from the right fountain, and therefore it could not but be pleasing to God.

This manner of the king's praying teaches us two further things. First, it assures us regarding his faith. Second, it assures us regarding his repentance. Otherwise, how can I crave anything from the hands of one whom I do not trust? Or, as the apostle says, how can we call on him in whom we do not believe?[13] Therefore, prayer to God is one evidence that we do trust in God. Thus I say, it is evidence of the king's faith, and where there is faith, of necessity repentance must also be present; for these two companions, faith and repentance,

---

[13] 'Whosoeuer beleueth in him, shal not be ashamed. ... But how shal thei call on him, in whome they haue not beleued? and how shal they beleue in him, of whome they haue not heard?' (Rom. 10:11, 14; Gen.B).

are inseparable as Peter testifies in Acts 15:9. For, so far as the heart is purged, so far is the life renewed; that is why faith and life go together.

Therefore, since his prayer is evidence of his faith, and his faith is evidence of his repentance, it follows that his repentance is evidence of the secret condition implicit in the prophet's solemn warning of his impending death: when the condition is fulfilled, the threat of death is removed. It appears by this reasoning that though the prophet spoke very explicitly, within the announcement of the king's death there was a condition applying to the king's response. So much then for Hezekiah's behaviour when he was struck down ill.

However, very briefly, consider also the king's gesture. We read in verse 2 that he turned his face to the wall. There is no question but that he did this for two reasons. First, that he might weep the more bitterly. For the next verse tells us that he poured forth his soul in tears, and we gather he did not want his anguish to be seen by others. Second, he turned his face to the wall so that his eyes should not look around him and distract his mind from God. For we know that whenever any one of us is praying in a public place, if we witness some incident, the event will draw our senses away from the communion that we are having with God. So it is expedient for all who would pray earnestly to withdraw to some secret place, just as our Master commanded his disciples to enter their private room. So much for the king's gesture.

The words of the king's prayer

In his prayer (we find it in verse 3) he does not bring to God his actual request (for his real petition is the prorogation[14] of his days); Daniel likewise 'suppresses' his real request in chapter 9:4-16.[15] Rather, both the king and Daniel give the reasons why their petition should be heard. Hezekiah offers three reasons. The first is, 'Remember, Lord, that I have walked in your truth.' Second, 'I have walked with an upright heart.' Third, 'I have done that which is good in your sight.' In all three it might appear that he is boasting of his own merits, for his words seem to be full of ostentation and pride. But the answer to such a suggestion is that the Lord does not measure ostentation and pride by words, but by the heart from which those words proceed. A broken, humble, and contrite heart is ever acceptable to him, whatever form of words is used. Likewise, a proud heart is ever displeasing to him, whatever form of words is used.

Now, what is the king doing here? He is not vaunting himself or bragging in the words he uses. Rather, he is seeking to show to God that, however serious his illness was, nevertheless his conscience was clear, and this testimony upheld him.[16] I mean, even if outward circumstances appeared to

[14] 'Prorogation of his days' is Bruce's actual phrase; he means 'the prolonging of his days'.

[15] Daniel's request in chapter 9:4ff. does not become apparent until verse 17.

[16] Bruce lays great stress on Hezekiah's conscience. To understand more fully the significance of this in Bruce's theological thinking, readers might care to study his teaching on 'Conscience' in the book, *The Mystery of the Lord's Supper*, tr. & ed. by T. F. Torrance, ch. 4, on 'Let a man examine himself, and so let him eat of that bread and drink of that

be saying that God was angry with him, yet he could not be persuaded in his conscience that God was not his friend. In effect, throughout his entire prayer it is as if he was saying this: 'Lord, you know that the godless men of this land will regard me as cursed if I die without children, and they will think all I have done until now to be accursed. They will blaspheme and condemn the religion that I have reformed and the re-ordering of worship in your house that I have begun. Nevertheless, I am clear in my conscience that all that I have done has been fully in accordance with your laws. I have not acted for myself, but only for you, O Lord.'

This kind of reasoning does not arise from either ostentation or pride. So he continues, as it were, 'Therefore, Lord, remember me, and do not take my life from me, lest I be a stumbling-block to the weak ones and a cause of jubilation to my enemies.' This is the main lesson for us here: we see how this good king, when all worldly comfort failed him and he was in his greatest extremity, reposed himself upon the testimony of his conscience. It was this that sustained and comforted him; nothing else; it was this, when he was at the very threshold of death, that he had to support him.

When I read through the Bible I find that all God's servants in their deepest troubles always had recourse to this testimony of a clear conscience.[17] You see Moses, when he had to do with Korah, Dathan and Abiram, having recourse to this testimony

---

cup', 1 Cor. 11:28 (London: James Clarke, 1958) pp. 139-156. A second imprint, including Kindle edition, is readily available (Fearn, Ross-shire: Christian Focus Publications, 2005). See also Appendix 1 below, p. 163.

[17] See note 16 above.

of his conscience.[18] You see David, when he had to do with Saul, also had recourse to this testimony of conscience.[19] You see Nehemiah having recourse to this.[20] You see Daniel having recourse to this (Dan. 6:22). And the apostle Paul in 1 Corinthians 4:3, 4: 'With me it is a very small thing that I should be judged by you or by any human court… I am not aware of anything against myself.' Paul's glory was the testimony of his own conscience. The author of the Letter to the Hebrews, in the last chapter, wrote, 'Pray for us, for we are sure that we have a clear conscience, desiring to act honourably in all things' (13:18). So go through all the servants of God, and you will see that they have always had recourse to this testimony of conscience; and blessed is that man who is not condemned by his own conscience in what he does. For if we are not able to avoid the condemnation of our own hearts, how shall we be able to avoid the condemnation of God who sees all the secrets of our heart? So whoever is not condemned by his own heart is never more blessed.

A further word about our consciences: they are able faithfully to keep us on the right path. The measure it receives is the measure that it renders in return. For good turns done it gives a happy testimony; but for evil turns it gives a bitter testimony. But just say that most of our deeds are concealed from human eyes, and the testimony of our consciences is mainly hidden from ourselves, yet there is a day coming, that

---

[18] 'Thē Moses waxed verie angrie, & said vnto the Lord, Loke not vnto their offring, I haue not taken so muche as an asse frō thē, nether haue I hurte anie of thē.' (Num. 16:15; GenB).

[19] 1 Sam. 24:13-15.

[20] Neh. 5:18-19; 11:22, 30-31.

even now is near, when everything presently hidden under the cloak of darkness shall come to light. Then the secrets of all our hearts will be revealed. The heavenly book of the records of consciences shall be opened, and whoever's sins are not recorded in the book as discharged, at the cost of the blood of Christ, shall be judged by the sentence of the righteous Judge. For whoever's guilty conscience is not cleansed of evil done during this life shall be condemned. And the whole company of angels, along with God's elect children, shall declare his judgment to be righteous. Therefore, it is time now to have registered in the heavenly book the discharge of all our sins.

Would to God that I might secure this discharge of all sins for the kirk's and government's office-bearers! O that now during their life-time they would obtain this, so that their consciences will be blameless when they come to die! The Lord grant this to all of those who seek to serve him, but specially, your majesty, may the Lord enable you so to conduct your life that you may have a joyful testimony of your conscience at your death. I pray your own conscience may be approved, and that God's own testimony of your conscience may be made sure in the mouths of the two faithful witnesses;[21] and that your salvation may be sure, not on your own account, but through the blood of Christ Jesus, whose mercy is our only merit.

As this is craved for our king, so it is craved for all who hold office. Lord, grant that they may pursue such a manner

---

[21] It would appear that Bruce is referring to the two witnesses of Rev. 11:3-4: 'But I wil giue power vnto my two witnesses ... These are two oliue trees, & two cãdel stickes, stãding before ye God of ye earth' (GenB).

of life that in their deaths their consciences may make joyful mention of how they have lived.

Turning for mercy to the one who opposed him

As I near my conclusion, there remains one further matter I must address. It is to do with Hezekiah's behaviour in a serious dilemma. On one side he is trapped by the serious nature of his disease; on the other side, he is hemmed in by God's solemn warning that he is to die. How does he react in these dire straits? He turns in prayer to the God who has smitten him, and who now through the prophet threatens him.

This is quite wonderful! For had he been dealing with any other person such as the king of Assyria who had only recently confronted him, it would have been an easy matter to turn to God. But now it is God who is confronting him, appearing to be opposing him; it is remarkable that he should have had recourse to his apparent assailant. This is noteworthy faith in this king. Hoping against hope, he ran to the very one who was challenging him. In spite of the fact that God was threatening him with death, he fled to him, and appealed for his justice and mercy through the merits of Christ. He appealed to him as to a righteous Judge and Redeemer in Christ, and his appeal was heard. For as we shall see later (God willing) Hezekiah was healed.

The king's prayer that he might live

Regarding the prorogation of his days, the question might rise whether it was appropriate[22] for him to crave it or not. I shall

---

[22] Bruce's word is 'leisom' which the Scots Lexicon defines as meaning 'pleasant, lovable, agreeable'. I have translated it as 'appropriate' which seems to carry the sense of what he means.

deal with this first in the case of the king. It was lawful for him to make this request because as yet he had no heir, and in this God's promise made to his father David had not yet been effected. Further, the reformation of the kirk[23] was only just begun, nor was the welfare of his people yet established, and both of these demanded Hezekiah's continued presence. In this regard, his prayer was certainly appropriate.

But speaking generally, I believe it would also be appropriate for others to pray for prolongation of their lives, because length of days is one of the greatest temporal blessing given to us; that is the promise attached to the fifth commandment. Also, the apostle wrote of the illness of Epaphroditus, 'Indeed he was ill near to death. But God had mercy on him, and not only on him but on me also, lest I should have sorrow upon sorrow' (Phil. 2:27). So Paul considered prolongation of days a special mercy. And there is no mercy or blessing of God that may not be craved, as long as it is for the right reasons. For we, directing our lives for God's glory, and living them as pilgrims and aliens seeking their true home, and if we are also always prepared to place them into God's hands as may be his will, why is it not appropriate to crave this blessing?

Jesus appears to contradict this when he says, 'Whoever loves his life loses it' (John 12:25). But that means that while there is a love of life that it to be commended, there is also a love of life which must be rebuked, namely an extraordinary love which places a person's entire welfare and happiness only in this life, without any thought or desire for the life to come. It is that love of life which Jesus condemns. But the other

[23] Contrary to the teaching in some Christian churches, reformed theology understood ethnic Israel to be the OT church.

love that is of God, is when we are prepared to place our lives wholly in the hands of his heavenly majesty, and seek the prolongation of our days solely for his glory. That is what the king did as he states clearly in verses 18 and 19. So much for our consideration of the king's petition.

Therefore, if we honour God and seek his glory, we too may ask this blessing. Yet always, please observe, that in his extremity the king's only consolation was that he had the testimony of a good conscience; and this ought also to uphold us when God afflicts us either with some serious illness or some other severe adversity.

Well, as I said at the beginning of this sermon, should afflictions from the Lord cause us truly to turn to him that he might cleanse our consciences here and now, then we should have as great a consolation in our troubles as did Hezekiah. Would to God that he would so soften our hearts!

The Lord work this in you, your majesty, that as he has honoured you in your birth you may honour him in the performance of your governing. May the Lord in his mercy give us all hearts to crave this. May the Lord give us hearts to grieve over those things we have not the will to mend. Lord, give us grace to turn wholly to Christ Jesus, that in his mercy we may at length enter the heavenly city. For outside it are but swine and dogs, Popery and idolatry. Let us, I say, turn wholly to this God who alone is able to preserve his kirk and our nation. To this God be all honour, praise, and glory, now and for ever. Amen.

The Second Sermon

Upon the 38th Chapter of the Prophecy of Isaiah

Preached in the Presence of the King's Majesty

Then the word of the LORD came to Isaiah: ⁵ 'Go and say to Hezekiah, Thus says the LORD, the God of David your father: I have heard your prayer; I have seen your tears. Behold, I will add fifteen years to your life. ⁶ I will deliver you and this city out of the hand of the king of Assyria, and will defend this city.'—Isaiah 38:4-6

IN our discussion of this king's disease we observed: First, the manner and nature of this disease. Second, we noted the time when it came upon him. Third, we noted the gravity of the disease. Finally, we thought about the way in which he reacted to this disease.

As to the nature of the disease, we saw that it was a purulent kind of boil similar to the plague of boils[1] in Egypt—a boil of the worst kind possible in those days. Thus it pleased

---

[1] The Scots word used here is 'botch'. See above, Sermon One, Note 1.

the Lord to try the faith of his dear servant; though he loved this king, it pleased him to deal with him very harshly. We remarked regarding this that God's favour and severity should not be judged by any worldly standards. Even though plagues and afflictions are visited upon both good and evil men, yet the cause for which they are sent is not the same, neither is the Lord's purpose the same in sending them. The Holy Spirit assures us that this kind of chastening is the only way to purge our iniquities, as, for example, in the case of Jacob. Therefore let no one think unkindly of his brother's sorrows on account of some affliction.

Second, we remarked on the time when the king contracted this illness as being in the fourteenth year of his reign, shortly after he had been delivered out of the hands of Sennacherib. Thus, just after having been saved from falling into an assailant's hands and a fearful war, he now falls into the hands of another assailant, a serious sickness. So we saw that the king's life was constantly fraught and in continuous trouble; no sooner had he escaped from one grave danger than an even greater threat came upon him; in other words, life for him was a persistent vexation.

We see, then, that the Lord was pleased to test the patience of his child in order that he might engender in him a discontent with this life so that he would set his heart on a far better life. The Lord does not treat his children as if they were calves being fattened for slaughter. No, but he constantly lays some cross on their backs so that they may learn to set their affections on things above; also, that they may learn how to use this earthly life and its fleeting trifles to prepare them for their heavenly lives. So much then for the timing of Hezekiah's affliction.

As for the gravity of his illness, we portrayed it in two of its aspects. First, it was terminal, for there was at that time no known means of healing it. Second, it was pronounced as incurable by the Lord's prophet, and this message must have greatly aggravated the suffering caused by the illness. From Isaiah's message we learn a lesson concerning the kindnesses and severity of God, namely, that in both there is attached an invariable condition that is here being applied to the king. The prophet's mission was not intended to reduce Hezekiah to despair, rather its purpose was to cause him the more earnestly to seek God's grace and mercy.

The final point we made in the first sermon was the lesson arising from the king's reaction to his affliction. We saw on the one hand that the sickness threatened him, yet on the other hand God was chastening him that he might have recourse to him as his Lord and Master. We also noted on the one hand that it had been obvious he should turn to God when the king of Assyria was threatening him, yet on the other hand that it was a wonderful triumph of faith he should have cast himself upon the Lord when it seemed it was he who was assailing him. He could never have acted thus had he not had the testimony of a good conscience.[2] How could he have ever turned to the God who is a consuming fire had his conscience been full of guilt! But because he was upheld by the testimony of a clear conscience he understood that the severity of God was to make him, not to break him.

Consequently, we framed this benediction, 'Blessed is the one who is not condemned by his conscience!' For if we cannot escape the condemnation of our hearts, how much

[2] On 'conscience' see above, Chapter One, Note 16.

less will we ever be able to escape the condemnation of God who sees and knows our hearts? For the Lord only condemns those who are themselves first condemned by their own consciences. That is why he has endowed us with consciences that we might be pre-warned of the coming judgment. For we are assured that when our consciences are clear according to his word, the Lord on that day will finally approve us.

We also saw that the application of this was that all who hold office[3] should so conduct themselves in their living that when they depart this life they too may have the testimony of a clear conscience. But that cannot happen unless each one changes entirely his daily conduct and keeps himself free from the sins of others. Therefore, I again exhort everyone, in whatever station you may be, from the greatest to the least, that the Lord by his Spirit should rule your conscience, you also, your Majesty, that you all may keep yourselves apart from the sin and iniquity around you. This, then, is how far we reached in the first sermon on this chapter.

Comfort from heaven sent to Hezekiah

The form and manner of the comfort sent to the king are recorded in the three verses of the text that I read. But the circumstances are given in greater detail in 2 Kings 20:4-6. (Note that here the order of verses 4 to 6 is the same as in Isaiah 38.) The writer uses verse 4 as a preface to inform us of the time and place this message was given, together with its author and the Lord's servant who was entrusted with it. In the next verse

[3] In the first sermon, office-bearers in both kirk and government were explicitly mentioned.

we have the narrative: the Lord had heard the king's prayer, seen his tears and now brought him comfort. Then in verse 6 we have the confirmation of this promise together with a wonderful sign and miracle from heaven.

The timing of this answer to prayer

We start, then, with Isaiah 38:4 where the timing is implied though not given explicitly: 'Then came the word of the Lord to Isaiah, saying… .' The word 'then' relates to the timing, which is set down more specifically in 2 Kings 20; there we learn that before the prophet had left the middle court God spoke to him and commanded him not to leave. See the short distance between the chamber where the king lay on his bed and the room next to it where Isaiah now stood; that was the same short distance between the prophet's first grim message and then its reversal. He was not yet out of the king's residence when the Lord told him to return and withdraw the pronouncement of death! The same lips that made the first announcement now make the contrary announcement. This sudden and wonderful change brings us to several notable points worthy of our consideration.

First, observe how forceful[4] and effectual the king's prayer had been, so effectual, indeed, that it moved the great God to overturn the death sentence that had been pronounced. What neither heaven, nor earth, nor any other creature was able to accomplish, the prayer of his own servant caused God to do for him. Even more, this prayer obtained bodily health,

---

[4] Bruce's word is 'pithie' which in Braid Scots can mean either, 'vigorous', 'forceful', 'concise' or 'terse'.

length of days, a sure and prosperous state, and added to all this was a miraculous confirmation the like of which was never seen or heard of before.[5]

See then—are the prayers of the faithful not wondrously effectual? Is it indeed possible that all these results can flow from prayer's pithiness[6], even though on its own there is nothing quite so futile as prayer?[7] Yet such effects of Hezekiah's prayer flow from the very nature of God's mercy, the compassion God has on our misery. When prayer is instantly heard, that is the only reason.

2 Second, here we may also learn how well God corresponds to the names given to him in Exodus 34:6,[8] where he declares himself to be a God of great compassion, and excelling in mercy towards us. Thus there are at times specific occasions when he instantly grants our requests.

3 Third, it has come home to me how direct and close is the connection between the faithful soul on earth on the one hand, and God in heaven on the other hand. This bond is so intimate that God is as present in our prayers as if heaven and earth were joined together. Similarly, this bond in prayer makes his Son Christ to be as near in our time of need as if he had placed his throne of grace in the bed where we lie. We can be certain of this when we consider how swiftly the

[5] Isa. 38:8.

[6] See Note 4 above.

[7] By prayer 'on its own', Bruce seems to mean (as in Shakespeare's *Hamlet*), 'My words fly up, my thoughts remain below; words without thoughts never to heaven go.'

[8] Exod. 34:6: 'So the Lord passed before his face, and cryed, The Lord, ye Lord, strong, merciful, and gracious, slow to angre, & abundant in goodness and trueth' (GenB).

king's prayer rose upwards, and how the answer came immediately, with such a rapidity that it seemed as if there was no
distance at all between earth and heaven. Therefore learn:
God is joined to the faithful soul as if there was no space at
all between heaven and earth; it is not as if God is in another
room to ours and it takes some time for him to get up and
come through to see us where we are waiting. Where there is
faith, there need be no delay before he receives our requests.
Those who think it necessary to have a priest to pray on their
behalf must not refuse this great truth because they cannot
understand it, for faith transcends our understanding. The
things of the Spirit cannot be judged by human reasoning.

The location of the answer to the king's prayer

As the prophet was commanded to turn back while he was in
the second hall,[9] clearly the king was still in his residence and
lying on his bed. And, incidentally, it was a great sign of the
favour of God towards him that he fell ill at home where he
could be cared for, without being hassled by others.

Concerning the location, there can be no doubt that the
author of this comfort was God himself, for every good gift
flows from him. God chose to use his own prophet to con-
vey and apply the comfort to the king, although that is not
to imply that he needed human help to do this. Rather, it
pleased the Lord to work by condescending to bind himself
to use Isaiah as his instrument, even binding himself to the
prophet's preaching; apart from this he chooses not to work.

[9] 2 Kings 20:4-5: 'And afore Isaiah was gone out into the middle of
the court, the worde of the Lord came to him, saying, Turne againe...'
(GenB).

33

That is why he calls his word a sword, a fire, a hammer, and an arrow, for his word is effective in varying ways. Thus, binding himself to his word, God willingly binds himself to his servants who minister his word.

He chooses to work only through those ministers to whom he has entrusted his word, for he does not bind himself to the words of any[10] whom he has not commissioned! Therefore those are quite wrong who think that by reading the Scriptures privately in their own homes they can derive as much benefit as from sermons. They argue that they have no need to listen to the word being preached because, they say, they can read better than their minister can preach. But that is not what the Scriptures teach: it is by hearing that faith comes, and so if they condemn the hearing they also condemn faith. God's means of faith is that the word should be preached and heard; this is his usual way of working, ordinarily.[11]

---

[10] The sense of Bruce's expression could be paraphrased as, 'God does not bind himself to the words of any Tom, Dick or Harry.' I hesitatingly refrained from using such a colloquial expression.

[11] Bruce's teaching here echoes Calvin: *Institutes* IV.1.5-6; also, 9: 'Wherever we see the Word of God purely preached and heard (*Dei verbum sincere praedicari atque audiri*), and the sacraments administered according to Christ's institution, there, it is not to be doubted, a church of God exists.' *The Scots Confession* (1560) does not add the words 'and heard' to the first of the 'three notes' of a true kirk: 'the Word of God truly preached, the Sacraments rightly administered, and discipline executed according to the Word of God, are certain and infallible signs of the true Kirk' (ch. 25; see also ch. 18). Bruce's adherence to the reformer's 'preached and heard' suggests he had been taught by someone who was familiar with Calvin's teaching, probably Andrew Melville. Though of course there had been translations into English of the *Institutes* by then that Bruce may well have read for himself.

The comfort[12] *Isaiah was commissioned to bring to the king*

We should note certain points about the comfort Hezekiah received. There were three ways in which the Lord's Word brought succour to him. The first two were direct answers to his prayer, namely, the healing of his body and the granting of length of days—fifteen more years. The third never entered his mind to request: a glorious and stable kingdom for the rest of his life; this was apparently far more than he had hoped for.

A comparison of the prefaces to the prophet's two messages

Before we consider the prophet's commission from God to the king, we should notice the manner in which these answers to prayer are introduced. 'Then the word of the LORD came to Isaiah: Go and say to Hezekiah, Thus says the LORD, the God of David your father.' This preface to the message differs in two ways from the original preface to God's first message in verse 1. First, David is not mentioned in the earlier preface. So why is the Lord called, 'the God of David your father'? Whenever David is referred to in any introduction to some message, we should understand that we are being reminded of the Lord's singular favour and mercy, and consequently we should think of Christ because David foreshadowed him. Thus the occurrence of David's name here is to let the king know that the swiftness of the succour being brought to him

---

[12] Bruce's word was 'comfort'. Readers should note that the verb 'to comfort' originally had the connotation of 'to strengthen' or 'to bring courage' (Latin, *con*, with + *fortis* courageous). The contemporary meaning of the noun 'comfort' as 'relief from anxiety' falls short of the sense of Bruce's 'comfort'; as Bruce used the word, it meant 'to bring succour or aid as well as consolation'.

flowed from the Messiah, Jesus Christ, from whom all true succour flows, and without whom there is neither aid nor consolation. That is why the Lord calls himself the God of David, because the principal promises of grace were made to David and his house, and especially that promise concerning the Messiah, in whom all other promises are 'yea and amen', and are fully accomplished in him. This is the first point of difference.

The second difference is that in this second preface to the divine message David is called the king's father. It is as if the Lord is saying to Hezekiah, 'That man whom I know and love so well I see to be your father, and you to be his child and son, not only by nature but also by grace. I recognize that you are his son in the faith, therefore all the promises of grace made to him and his descendents must rightly apply also to you. Otherwise, had you simply been his son by natural descent, those promises of grace would no more have pertained to you than they did to your father Ahaz.' It is as the apostle has written in Romans 9, 'It is not the children of the flesh who are the children of God… For not all who are descended from Israel belong to Israel… but the children of the promise are counted as offspring' (verses 6 and 8).[13] In other words, those who through faith in the promise of mercy become the sons of mercy, are made the children of God. Therefore, this faith in God's promises not only makes us his sons, but also sons of David and Abraham. For as by faith we follow in the footsteps of Abraham and imitate his faith, we become his sons.

[13] Bruce seems to be quoting from memory as he begins the citation from Rom. 9 at verse 8, then reverts to verse 6, before returning to verse 8.

Isaiah's obedience

We need to take note of certain points regarding Isaiah's second message here in verses 5 and 6. After the prophet had delivered his first message (verse 1), he did not delay or remain in the king's residence, but at once began to leave—that is, until God spoke to him again, this time commanding him to stand still and remain in the palace. For God had a special commission for him before he departed. This teaches every minister and office-bearer in God's service that no one should engage in any action at his own instigation, but before he proceeds to his task he must have the Lord's own warrant which must come from his word.

The other point concerning the second message is that as soon as God spoke to him he obeyed. He did not dither or doubt or question the Lord, but instantly acted on his word. Think about it: if ever any mortal man had every reason to complain, it was Isaiah. Why? Almost immediately he was commanded to reverse that first grim message he had just delivered and to declare to the king the very opposite. Obedient to the Spirit, he obeyed.

Such an unexpected and sudden about-turn might have raised serious doubts and questions in the king's mind regarding the first message. Had Isaiah been as angry and disgruntled as Jonah, he would undoubtedly have questioned God's word. Remember how Jonah had not been commanded by God to reverse his message; yet, when the judgment he had prophesied never took place, he fretted and fumed against God. Indeed, had he been instructed suddenly to go and withdraw the threat of judgment, we can easily conjecture what his reaction would have been. Jonah's angry state of mind tells us that he was ignorant of the nature of God's solemn warnings, for had he known that always they are conditional and that God is not willing that any should perish but that all should repent, he would not have reacted so angrily against the Lord's mercy upon a penitent people. That was why he fell into such fuming and fretting against God.

Two lessons from Isaiah's obedience

There are two lessons here for those who teach God's word. The first is to avoid Jonah's wrong attitude. He was so concerned about his own reputation that he raged against God's mercy! All who hold office in God's church should take careful note. God still directs the most solemn warnings against sacrilegious men whose evil hands are stained with the blood of those they oppress. But I am sure that there is no office-bearer in the kirk who has the fear of God in his heart who would not greatly rejoice to see such threatenings turned completely round in mercy. I am also assured that there is not a spiritual office-bearer with the fear of God in his heart who likewise would not rejoice to see all the solemn admonitions directed from this pulpit against magistrates of all ranks, from the highest to the lowest, turned about in divine mercy. Those who find it exceedingly hard and painful to deliver warnings of divine judgment are a thousand times more ready to share the comforts of the gospel when so commanded by the Holy Spirit.

Therefore, your majesty, the Lord in his mercy give you grace that you may have that consolation of a good conscience to uphold you, without which there is no real peace of mind and heart. Nevertheless, sire, when I look upon the misery and calamity of this nation, I almost lose hope. Your subjects have fallen into such hardness of heart that nothing pleases them but those things that displease God, and what pleases him displeases them. I ask you, what is it that renders habitual practice almost impossible to change? What is it that constant usage does not harden? For example, some food when first tried seems to have an unpleasant taste, but when it is often eaten it becomes tolerable. Continue to eat it and the bitter taste appears to go away. Keep on eating it and ultimately it seems to be quite sweet and you cannot understand why at first it had such a bad taste.

That is what happens to an evil man who begins to find pleasure in doing evil; he ultimately develops such a taste for wickedness that what he constantly enjoys doing is displeasing to God, and what is pleasing to God displeases him. The habitual practice of wrong-doing banishes light from a man's mind, and that in turn obliterates the light of his conscience. Light is replaced by darkness and so a once sensitive soul is corrupted by a conscience that has been seared. All that remains in such a person is a wicked and obdurate state of mind that resembles the devil's who is said to be bound in chains and in perpetual darkness.[14]

Inexplicably, no repeated thundering of the impending divine judgment is able to move them, neither is any preaching able to touch them. No! Once a man has given himself

---

[14] The allusion is to Rev. 20:1-3: 'And I sawe an Angel come downe from heauen, hauing the keye of the bottomles pit, and a great chaine in his hand. And he toke the dragon that olde serpēt, which is the deuil and Satan, and he bounde him a thousand yeres. And cast him into the bottomless pit, and he shut him vp, and sealed the dore vpon him …' (GenB).

over to wickedness and dishonesty he cannot help himself. For once sin has mastered such men, as Peter says, it rules them more completely than any prince would rule his subjects.[15] Therefore, sire, I pray that God may so abundantly bestow on you the gift of government—that holy unction of kingship—that we may begin to see this proud insolence of so many, that manifests itself in such contempt of righteousness, justly punished in order that you too may maintain a pure and holy conscience. So much for what must at all costs be avoided.

The second lesson from Isaiah's obedience arises from his readiness to say what the Lord commanded him. When the Lord bade him to blow the blast of judgment, he blew it; when the Lord bade him to come, he came; when the Lord bade him to go, he went. The lesson for those of us who preach is this: we may not blow the trumpet to please either ourselves or our hearers, but only as the Lord bids us. We may not sound the retreat when we should sound the advance, nor dare we sound the advance when we should sound the retreat. Neither may we sound out judgment when the Lord bids us sound out mercy, nor may we sound out mercy when the Lord bids us sound out judgment.

Today, the sins of our land demand that every pulpit should be sounding out judgment. Therefore judgment must be sounded! There is only one way to avert this judgment and that is when every single person, whatever his status or position, wholeheartedly supports the reformation, inasmuch

[15] Bruce's allusion may to be to 2 Pet. 2:19: 'Promising vnto them libertie, and are them selues the seruants of corruption: for of whome soeuer a man is ouercome, euen vnto the same is he in bondage' (GenB).

40

as it lies within his power so to do. The best way forward must be for you present today who are nobles to concur with your prince, and that his majesty also concur with heart and hand to repair the ruins of our nation. So much for this second lesson.

The Lord's answer to the king's prayer

We next read that Isaiah said to the king that the Lord had heard his prayer and had seen his tears. It is as if he said, 'Even though you were lying in your bed-chamber, your face turned to the wall, I heard every word you spoke and saw the tears flowing down your cheeks; even though you were not praying in the temple, I saw and heard everything.' Herein is surely great consolation: in all places, for rich and poor alike, the Lord's ear is ever open to the cries of his own, seeing their sorrow and hearing their words. Even though he does not answer as swiftly as he answered Hezekiah, nonetheless, he does not leave them; rather, in the meantime he sustains them by his Spirit until ultimately he does answer in the manner that is appropriate for them. Indeed, if it is his will for them, he gives them even more than they asked for.

If the Lord's ear is open to the prayers of his own children and his eyes see their tears, then will he not also be moved by the cries of those who are oppressed by evil men who do not scruple to shed blood? Although such men remain unmoved by every threatening and denunciation, since every word is heard by the Lord and all tears are poured into his vial, how much more shall every drop of blood spilled by these men also be there in that divine vial? Why will these men not give ear? They have taken their stance on shifting sand and on that false foundation they build their conclusions, as do the atheists, that there is no God; on this same foundation are enacted out all their evil deeds. They have tried to rid their minds of any knowledge of God, their consciences of any vestiges of feelings and their hearts of all that might give them anxiety. But I ask those who have joined the company of atheists, if there is no God, how is it their consciences continue to trouble them? The truth is that secret fears and inner disquiet gnaw at their hearts; nor can they wholly banish this foreboding. But if they deny God exists, why are they so tormented? The more murders they commit as a means of ridding themselves of those who trouble them, ever more intense is the fear in their hearts.

So where does this disturbing apprehension come from, if not from God warning them of the wrath to come, and telling them that they are already experiencing the beginnings of hell here in this life? Truly, if God were to give them a sense of the full measure of eternal punishment, they would attempt to end their own lives by some violent means in the forlorn hope that for their souls to be separated from their bodies might prove a means of escape from the increasing ugly pains and ever greater torments in their hearts. Tragically, although these pains and torments consume them, they do not move them to repentance; the Lord alone could work that in them. He commands all to hear his word and has promised to work through his servants who speak that word. That is why these oppressors and men of blood ought to be present among us today so that the Lord, if it be possible, might bring them to repentance. That is the only way they can be saved from that terrible judgment for which they have at present just a slight forewarning. Yet, before they depart this life, that forewarning in their souls will be much more ominous.

The implications arising from the comfort brought to the king

Before I conclude, I return to what I mentioned earlier, namely, the comfort Hezekiah received. We saw that there were three ways in which the Lord's word brought succour to him. The first two were answers to his prayer, the third was more than he asked. His sickness healed and his years prolonged were both what he prayed for. Also granted him and which he did not expect was a glorious and stable kingdom: the Lord would not only deliver him out of the hands of the king of Assyria, but would also deliver the fortified cities. Much could be said about this, but now I only want you to observe one point.

In granting the king more than he requested and thus causing him to be grateful throughout the coming years, God sought to guide him in this way: 'Whatever you lack, seek it from me. Do you need good health? Seek it from me. Do you desire length of days? Seek it from me. Do you long for a glorious and prosperous kingdom? Seek it from me.' There could not be a more kindly approach of God to the king, for he desired that whatever Hezekiah lacked, he should ask it from the Lord.

If kings do not resolve to honour God that he might constantly extend his grace to them, it would never be possible for them to expect him to bless them as he blessed Hezekiah. On the other hand, if kings determine to serve God that he might extend his favour towards them, there is no honour or dignity that he will not provide for them, by their birthright or in other ways. Whatever he sees is good and fitting for them, even if it vexes other nations, those kings shall enjoy the use and possession of whatever God gives. But if they fall away from serving God and so cast themselves out of his favour, they shall lose their dignity, birthright, the privileges of their heredity and everything else, plus their own selves.

Examples of this are in the Scriptures. Cain, Adam's eldest son, had the birthright as long as he kept himself in God's favour; but when he lost that favour by killing his brother Abel, he was banished from God's presence and forfeited his birthright and his entire heritage. Ishmael was also an older son, yet because he did not enjoy God's favour, he received no inheritance from Abraham. Esau also was his father's elder son, but because he too fell from God's favour his brother was preferred before him, his birthright counting for nothing.

The principle is this. It is only by the favour of God that men enjoy privileges, dignities, or whatever they may have a right to. As long as they remain in that favour, they will never be disappointed. Therefore this exhortation is easy for you, sire. As your majesty expects to retain and enjoy all that the Lord has appointed for you, so be sure to remain in God's favour. And the way to do this is to purge your nation of idolatry and the false teaching that the wine of the sacrament turns into blood; for under these two sins I take in all the sins committed against the two tables of the law. Accomplish this and it is certain that you will be blessed with all that is good and fitting for you. For the favour of God shall enable you to enjoy, not only your possessions, but all other privileges that you are born to. The Lord in his mercy work it in your heart, sire, that we may witness this as evidence of his favour when you resolve to reform our land, and so make it known that you fear God and love his people. This being done, even though men can be both unfaithful and deceitful, God is not a man, nor born of a man, that he should ever lie. Depend wholly on him. The Lord so work in all our hearts that we may earnestly crave and lay hold on this, that, our hearts being established by grace, we may obey God's holy will. The Lord grant it for Christ's sake, to whom be all honour, praise, and glory, for now and for ever. Amen.

The Third Sermon

Upon Isaiah Chapter 38

'This shall be the sign to you from the LORD, that the LORD will do this thing that he has promised: ⁸ Behold, I will make the shadow cast by the declining sun on the dial of Ahaz turn back ten steps.' So the sun turned back on the dial the ten steps by which it had declined.

⁹A writing of Hezekiah king of Judah, after he had been sick and had recovered from his sickness:

¹⁰ I said, In the middle of my days I must depart; I am consigned to the gates of Sheol for the rest of my years. ¹¹I said, I shall not see the LORD, the LORD in the land of the living; I shall look on man no more among the inhabitants of the world.—Isaiah 38:7-11

IN the last sermon, well-beloved in Christ, we learned of the manner and form of the comfort that was brought by the prophet to the sick king. We saw when it was delivered and where; we noted the person who gave it and the messenger who carried it; we considered the preface whereby the Lord

47

ensured the king's full attention; and we briefly thought about the content of the message and some aspects of the comfort that it offered. As to the circumstances, we noted where the prophet was when he received this commission: he was in the mid-court, not yet through the second hall, when the Lord's word bade him stay in the king's residence and return to the royal bed-chamber.

Now he was commanded to reverse the former message, and with that same mouth to pronounce the complete opposite. There was no more distance between the first sentence he spoke and this second sentence than there was between the king's private apartment and the room next to it. The brief time the prophet spent leaving the king's bedside and entering the second court was the same time between his first words and his second announcement.

Regarding the rapidity of this about-turn, we marked several notable points. First, the intensity of the king's prayer: it was so effectual that it moved the Lord to reverse his own sentence in a matter of seconds. What neither heaven nor earth nor any living being could have accomplished, this prayer of his servant moved him to do. As well as that retraction, the fervour of his prayer issued in the healing of his body, the prolonging of his life and the assurance of a prosperous and secure kingdom. We noted also the confirmation of God's promises by an amazing sign the like of which had neither been heard of nor seen before. Judge then for yourselves the power and effectiveness of a faithful man's prayer!

Second, I pointed out the wonderful inclination that the Lord has towards mercy, and how perfectly he answers to his names and titles as a God of great compassion and of exceeding and amazing kindness.

The third thing we noted arising from the swiftness of this answer to prayer was the closeness of the conjunction between the faithful soul on the one hand, and the Lord God on the other hand; indeed, so intimate is this bond that God is as near to the faithful soul as if heaven and earth were joined together. It means that by faith Christ, our helper, is as near to us in our hour of need as if he was seated on his throne of grace at the side of the bed where we are lying. Therefore, it is quite clear that no physical or geographical distance can ever impede the Lord in receiving and answering our prayers. The thickness of the walls of the room where the faithful soul is praying cannot keep out Christ's presence, for he is even closer to those who love him than any material object that may be right beside us.

We also noticed the significance of where the king was on this occasion—lying in his own bed. This was another indication of God's favour that he should fall ill when he was in his own residence, so not causing others hassle; this was God's gracious timing, for every good gift flows from him. We thought too of the Lord's messenger, Isaiah. Not that God needed him, for the Lord is not restricted in his working to any human instrument; rather that God freely wills to condescend to use such instruments to work through them to display his power.

At this point in my exhortation, I bade you to be diligent hearers of his word, and not to deceive yourselves with foolish conceit such as, 'I can read just as well at home, even better.' I repeat, the Lord will not work through your reading if you are despising his chosen method of working. God has bound himself to human instruments whom he has appointed in order that by hearing faith should come. He works in us by his Spirit when we hear his word. Listen to his word, therefore, as long as he continues to give you grace so to do. Do not despise the preaching of his word.

Regarding the preface to the second message brought to king ('Thus says the LORD, the God of David your father'[1]), we noted two points. First, David is now mentioned, whereas in Isaiah's first pronouncement in verse 1, his name did not occur. This reference to 'David your father' implicitly points to Christ, who alone was the source of the needed comfort, for in him all the promises of the Old Testament are grounded, and without him there is no true strength and consolation. Second, the phrase 'the God of David your father' is designating the king as David's son, not only by natural descent but also by grace. Therefore, all the promises of grace given to David justly appertained to Hezekiah; otherwise, without that grace, those promises would no more have applied to him than they did to his wicked father Ahaz. But through grace he was a son of grace and the possessor of the promises of grace. Thus it is clear that we are not children of God by natural descent, even though our parents were faithful souls but, as we follow in their faith, we become God's children through the promises of grace, and by this means we are joined to the company of all the faithful who have gone before.

Continuing with the second message, in my previous sermon we observed a further two points. First, Isaiah did not return until he was so commanded. The lesson to officebearers in the kirk was that they should not embark on any

[1] See 2 Kings 18:3.

course of action in their service to God until he gives the command. Second, we saw in Isaiah an outstanding example of willing obedience to the Lord. The prophet's first commission was a dire threatening, but in an instant it was reversed into a message of mercy; yet he was not angry or frustrated by this about-turn, but rejoiced to witness God's kindly dealings with the king.

Herein was another lesson for preachers: they should not be vexed when they see the Lord's threatenings suddenly turned around into the assurance of mercy. Of course everyone who teaches God's word accepts the justice of awesome warnings against murderers, adulterers, oppressors, and the sacrilegious. On the other hand, there is not a preacher who would not rejoice to see the Lord so evidently at work that he was called upon to minister comfort as well as to proclaim solemn warnings. The same principle holds true of magistrates: we all accept the rightness of stern justice being administered on evil men who have shed innocent blood; on the other hand, who will not be glad to see justice being tempered with mercy when the offence is only slight. Yet what prospect is there for mercy to be shown when iniquity increases among us so much that it exceeds all bounds? Surely then the Lord in heaven himself will take action if the magistrate fails to do his duty.

But to return to Isaiah: he had to sound the trumpet call of mercy when he was so bidden, and to sound judgment when that was bidden. For since the Lord has appointed us to be his mouth-pieces, we may not say whatever we may want, otherwise we would cease to speak for God and would be speaking only for ourselves. So whoever takes it upon himself to act as the Lord's mouth, let him sound out from the pulpit whatever the Lord bids him to sound.

In the text God says he had heard the king's prayer. In the same way, so he also hears the prayers and sees the tears of the oppressed in our land—our magistrates should likewise hear and see oppression. And as the Lord hears he gathers into his vial their tears; in his perfect time he will provide a remedy.

Finally, last time we saw that God offered the king three answers: healing of his body, length of days, together with a blessing that the king never prayed for, namely, a secure and prosperous state. Therefore, I exhorted our king who was present, and every one of you, to seek from God whatever you rightly desire, to seek it in Christ Jesus, whether it be for your body or your soul, for in him there are abundant riches for both. Provided you abide within God's favour and remain under his protection, nothing shall harm you. Nevertheless, the contrary holds true that if you step outside of his favour, you will lose all. This far we reached in my last study with you.

Our text for today

In the words that I have just read we have the confirmation of all that had been said to the king. And now it is made absolutely certain that what has been promised shall most surely take place. And as a guarantee God gives the king a truly amazing sign, the like of which had never been heard of or seen before. How did this come about? First, note that the king asked for a sign.[2] Then second, see that thereupon

[2] 2 Kings 20:8: 'For Hezekiah had said vnto Isaiah, What shalbe the signe be that the Lord wil heale me, and that I shal go vp into the house of the Lord the third day?' (GenB).

the Lord granted a sign. Third, the sign is given and made manifest, not by the ability of the prophet but by the power of God.

We begin then with the king asking for a sign (as may be seen in 2 Kings 20). And surely, in making this request, he did no wrong for when we look at the context and the history, it is clear he genuinely needed some sign. Commenting on miracles in the Scriptures and on this passage in particular, Augustine writes that because the prophet made two quite contrary statements within the space of less than an hour, clearly they could not both be fulfilled; therefore, it was right that a sign be given to confirm Isaiah's second pronouncement. It was as if the king said to the prophet, 'You came a little time ago and told me I was about to die; then a short time later you returned and said that I would live. How can I know this latter statement is true, and what token of its truth can I be given?' Was a sign necessary then? Surely, it was!

As to his soliciting for such a sign, he did not seek it out of unbelief, therefore he was not tempting God; rather he sought it to strengthen and confirm his weak faith—and is not all our faith similarly weak? The fact that our faith is often weak does not mean it is not true faith; if our faith is true and living, even though it is often weak, it is nonetheless genuine faith. However small the measure of our faith, it must be truly living; yet while we remain here in this world it cannot help but be weak.

Back then to Hezekiah: because his weak faith had to be strengthened, he needed some sign; I do not doubt he was constrained by the Holy Spirit so to ask. We read in Matthew that the wicked sought signs,[3] but the hearts of those who sought signs were void of faith. They did not seek them to confirm faith, for they had no faith to confirm; but they sought them out of unbelief and contempt of God. There is yet another possible reaction to a sign: an even harder heart of unbelief! For example, after Ahaz, Hezekiah's father, had been defeated by the Arameans, his army was again roundly defeated by Pekah, king of Israel; but Oded the prophet met the returning victors and had them send back to Judah the prisoners they had taken. But this sign from God did not soften the heart of Ahaz; instead we read that in his time of trouble he became even more unfaithful to the Lord. The sign had been no better than dung thrown at him; he cast it to one side as if he simply needed a change of clothing.[4]

His son Hezekiah was completely different. Following the example of god-fearing men before him, he longed for his faith to be confirmed. We read in Judges 6:17-22 that Gideon had asked for a sign. Earlier, Moses had sought a sign also for the strengthening of his faith.[5] Therefore in seeking a sign Hezekiah did nothing amiss, the proof of which is that God granted what he asked. Indeed, the Lord even gave him two options from which to choose and when he chose the more difficult of the two, humanly speaking, the Lord granted it to him.[6]

So what was this sign the Lord granted to him? The king

[3] Matthew 12:39: 'An euil and adulterous generacion seketh a signe ...' (GenB).

[4] See 2 Chron. 28.

[5] Exod. 3:11-12; 4:1-9.

[6] 2 Kings 20:8-11.

asked not only that the shadow of the degrees whereby the hours were registered on the palace's horologe, Ahaz's dial,[7] should be brought back, but also that he should observe the sun's backward movement. There had apparently already been ten hours of daylight, so that sunset was only two hours away. Count these hours: start with the twelve hours sunlight for that day, then add the additional ten hours when the sun's shadow all of an instant moved back, and then add the remaining two hours before sunset: we find that twelve hours were replaced by twenty-four hours! Was this not a most amazing event!

So the wonder of this sign was revealed, first, partly through the palace's horologe, which measured the sun's shadow and, second, partly through the sun's movement in the heavens recognized by the shadow on the steps. Regarding the former, it lets us see that the means men devise for measuring times and seasons together with the skill of those who invent and fashion them are not displeasing to God. It lets us know that long ago in the days of king Ahaz, they had invented a method of discerning the hour of the day. We too are able to follow the course of each day as morning, noon and evening; also of the night, midnight and cockcrow. But in our day, science has brought to us much more accurate means of telling

---

[7] Isa. 38:8: 'whereby it is gone downe in ye dial of Ahaz by the sunne' (GenB). Bruce's word 'horologe', which means in English today 'any device for telling the time', meant in sixteenth-century Scots 'a dial' as Heb. *ma'ala* 'a step or grade-mark' is translated by the English versions from Geneva Bible on. From about 2000 B.C., several kinds of sun-dials were in use in the Middle East, but because they could not register shadows when the sky was cloudy, by 1500 B.C. the Egyptians had invented water clocks; it might be to any of these that Bruce is referring.

the time than in the days of Ahaz and Hezekiah.[8] There is no record I know of that tells us the instruments used in Hezekiah's day were known in Greece until Anaximedes Milesius introduced them.[9] Neither is there any known record of them in Rome until they were introduced by Marcus Valerius Messalla[10] who brought them from a city called Catine in Sicilia.[11] Later, it was Marcus Varro[12] who brought to Rome the most advanced horologe in ancient times.[13] I am not attaching any importance to such particulars, so let us pass on to the sign's lessons for us in our faith in God.

Because it was visible on the face of the horologe that was

[8] The first mechanical clockmakers were known to have been in England in 1328; small domestic table clocks were in use by 1500; three working table clocks made by Bartholomew Newson in the 1580s still survive, one of which was recently on display (2013) as part of the exhibition of Mary Queen of Scots at the National Museum of Scotland in Edinburgh.

[9] Anaximedes of Miletus (585–528 BC) was a pre-Socratic Greek philosopher who reasoned that the *arche*, the underlying material of the world, was mainly air, which was the primary substance from which all things are made.

[10] There were at least ten Romans of that name; Bruce may be referring to a Marcus Valerius Messalla who was a Roman Republic consul in 226 BC

[11] Catine, now called Catania, is the second largest city in Sicily; founded in the 8th century BC it has had a long and eventful history. Today it is a centre of arts, education and industry.

[12] Marcus Terentius Varro (116–27 BC) was a notable Roman scholar whose interests centred on grammar, rhetoric, logic, arithmetic, geometry, astronomy, musical theory, medicine and architecture, which nine subjects became known as the 'liberal arts'; he is known to have written more than seventy-four books in Latin.

[13] I have retained Bruce's allusions to horology as they amply illustrate his classical scholarship.

set up in a public place at the top of the steps to the palace which was situated within sight of the temple to which the whole population resorted, this sign was witnessed by many people and so would have been known throughout all Judea. But also it was seen in the sun's movement in the heavens, and must therefore have been witnessed by all the world as well as by the people of Judah. People must have been stupefied to see such astounding evidence of God, whose divine person, in spite of his wonderful works in nature, is not visible to human eyes. Some may well have said to themselves, 'We are on the wrong pathway. We have been worshipping false gods and have forsaken the one true God.'

Surely, as I consider the wonders that God wrought from time to time on behalf of this king, I am constrained to think God purposely brought him into these dire extremities and dangers so that through these wonderful deliverances he might be known to the whole world. He led him into the kind of perils from which no human means could offer help; but God miraculously stepped in to deliver him by such wonders as made the whole world pause to think.

Another of God's purposes in this was that others should honour a man whom God himself had honoured, for it is only right that whom God honours, we too should honour. We know of other instances of God's miraculous intervention for this king such as when one night the Lord's angel put to death a hundred and eighty-five thousand men in the Assyrian camp.[14] And now, when the king had fallen into an incurable sickness with no one able to help him, the Lord wonderfully healed and confirmed this wonder by another

[14] 2 Kings 19:35.

wonder, the like of which had never been heard of before. It is true that in Joshua's time that the sun stood still in the heavens; but for the sun to go back by ten hours was unheard of. Look then! Did not these signs serve to honour God, and under him to honour his servant?

The profit to be gathered from signs

The benefit to be gathered from signs—I mean genuine signs that are clearly instigated by God—is to be found in what they represent; there is no genuine sign that does not have a clear message implicit within it. As Augustine has commented, for a sign to be genuine there must be within it some 'conformity and proportion' as there are in the sacraments. But the sign we are considering is not at all like the sacraments, for it is both miraculous and supernatural. Nevertheless, there may be uncovered within it some hidden relationship, for it is clearly evident that God would have us see, and the king also see, how easy it was for him to move back the sun's shadow by ten steps; although that was an easy thing for God to do, it was far easier for him to restore the king's health, and to give him back his life when he had been but a couple of hours from his death, indeed, snatched from its very jaws and brought into the fresh morning of joyful youth. For God both miracles— the king's healing and the sun's backward movement—were equally easy.

So how do such signs and wonders relate to Christ in the establishment of the new covenant? God's purpose, no doubt, is to strengthen the faith that we have already received through the preaching of the gospel. For signs are not given to create faith in Christ; faith is born through the preaching of the gospel. Signs are given as seals that confirm and enlarge our relationship with Christ. It is just as the apostle has written in Hebrews 2 that signs serve two ends: first, to bear witness to the truth and, second, to confirm the faith of the believer.[15] We see this clearly in the sacrament of the Supper, which was not instituted to create our faith in Christ. For we are not initially joined to Christ by this sacrament, rather it enables us to lay hold on Christ to whom we are already joined in some measure. The Lord's Supper is the means by which we possess Christ more wholly by extending the bounds of our narrow hearts so that he may be more fully received by us. This sign given to Hezekiah, therefore, offers some strength and comfort to us.

I acknowledge that there is greater blessing to be had from the preaching of the word than in the sign, and even greater blessing and strength than either of them through the Spirit's work within us. Nonetheless, each of these brings to the believer its own particular blessing. Although I maintain that the Holy Spirit can bring greater blessing than the word, yet the word must retain its own essential role in strengthening and comforting the believer. Yet there is no word able to express or heart able to receive even half of a quarter of the goodness and consolation that God has prepared for those who love him. In short, though the sign cannot bring as great

[15] Heb. 2:2-4: 'For if the worde spoken by Angels was stedfaste, and euerie transgression, and disobedience receiued a iuste recompense of rewarde, How shal we escape, if we neglect so great saluation, which at the first began to be preached by the Lord, and afterwarde was confirmed vnto vs by them that heard him, God bearing witnes thereto, bothe with signes and wonders, & with diuers miracles, and giftes of the holie Gost, according to his owne wil?' (GenB).

comfort as that brought to us through the word, yet it has its place in confirming the believer.

The prophet's role in the sign

I have already pointed out two aspects of the sign given: the first concerned the shadow registered on the public horologe, and the second concerned the sun's backward movement. But a third point remains to be noted. In the release of this sign, neither virtue nor power flowed out of Isaiah.[16] For it is said, 'This is the sign given of the Lord' (verse 7). Be sure of this: it is certain that there is no force or virtue in any creature, not even in the devil himself, that is able to work any genuine miracle; that belongs to God alone. Why? Every sign that is genuinely miraculous transcends the compass and bounds of nature. And no created being is able to do that and change the very parameters of their existence. Therefore all these supposed wonders assumed to be performed by satanic power, together with those claimed to be performed by pope and priests, are fraudulent and untrue. I am not stating this on my own authority, but on that of the apostle who wrote in 2 Thessalonians 2:9-10 that the appearance of the Antichrist shall be in the mighty power of the devil with false wonders and lying signs and with wicked deception. There is so much in entrances and porches of the Roman Catholic churches, so-called relics, and other objects, even arms and legs, which are manifestly lies and deceits of Satan.

---

[16] Bruce probably uses the word 'vertue' in an allusion to Mark 5:30: 'And immediatly when Iesus did knowe in him self the vertue that wēt out of him, he turned him roûde about in the preasse, and said, Who hathe touched my clothes?' (GenB).

Prayer the means of procuring the sign

As to the means whereby this sign was granted, we learn in 2 Kings 20[17] that it was procured by the prophet's prayer, for we read that he asked that the sun should move back; that clearly means Isaiah's prayer was made before the miracle occurred. We are to understand that it was the Lord's purpose to grant this sign, but he was going to give it through the prophet's prayer. The significance of this is that there is no intrinsic merit in our prayers, no power or virtue in our prayers to accomplish anything, but only what the Lord himself has willed to grant and that he will freely perform.

You ask, 'If that is so, then why should we pray?' We pray because prayer is part of the honour of God. He would have us be aware of our need of his benefits. He would have us engage in the exercise of prayer as part of our obedience to him. Therefore, when he does answer our prayers, so much the more will we ascribe all the glory to him.

We have recently had an outstanding example of the manifest effects of prayer. For through the prayers of our land and not least of this town's kirk, the Lord's threatening—in particular that fearful latest threatening of the vast armada of ships[18]—has been dramatically withdrawn. Alas, what honour have we ascribed to the Lord arising from that deliverance? How has it affected people's behaviour? When we consider the growth of wickedness since that brute of a navy was scattered, even more detestable sins are being committed among

---

[17] 2 Kings 20:11: 'And Isaiah the Prophet called vnto the Lord, and he broght againe the shadowe tē degrees backe by the degrees whereby it had gone downe in the dial of Ahaz' (GenB).

[18] The allusion is to the defeat of the Spanish Armada in 1588.

our people. Therefore, if anyone thinks that the Lord has withdrawn his hand because he did not smite us at that time, he must be either mad or devoid of any understanding or awareness of the divine intervention. Indeed, the Lord has temporarily withdrawn his hand, that we should learn the power of prayer and so that he might see how we will use the benefits he has given to us. But since his favour has been so greatly abused, and the only outcome is that our land is now burdened by a flood of iniquity plus the assumption that he has now been deprived of any means of punishing those who commit and direct these evil deeds, the Lord himself will surely act directly from heaven to punish us, or else he will spew our people out of his mouth. Even though the Lord should spare us, he will not forgive this contempt; and if he does, it will only be on account of his longsuffering. He allows men to heap up their sins against the day of his wrath.

Hezekiah's gratitude

There now follows in the scripture passage the record of the king's thankfulness to the Lord for the favour he had received. Indeed, the king is so thankful that he has recorded his song of gratitude which bears witness to the fact that he was not at all like many of us. So noteworthy is this song of lamentation and thanksgiving that there is none other like it from the pen of a king other than that in Psalm 51. First comes his lamentation regarding his infirmity and sickness; that is followed by his song of praise testifying of his gratitude to God.

The song is in three parts. In the first part he lets us see the great trial and perplexity into which he had been cast, and what he said and did in his trouble. In the second part he gives an account of all the great benefits he had received and how he promised to put his trust in God and depend on no other. In the third part he tells us that he will remember to be grateful as long as he lives, and to praise God all of his days and that he will never forget him.

Before we turn to the first part of Hezekiah's song, we need to have an overview of this king's life and the way he reacted down the years. Some of you might be unwilling to fall into step with other believers; if that is so, as you reflect on this king's life, you might be minded to learn from him. Pay attention then to some of the events of Hezekiah's life. In the fourteenth year of his reign, his cities were first attacked and then he was taunted by the king of Assyria's two ambassadors, the Rab-saris and Rabshakeh.[19] The Lord his God and he himself were mocked with the townspeople on the city walls listening in silence.[20] In this great extremity what did the king do? He turned to Isaiah the prophet that both of them might repair to the kirk to pray; that is the first thing that he did. When their prayers were the means of a wonderful deliverance, what then did he do? His prayer was for the glory and honour of God. So we see that prayer and praise were his chief spiritual exercises.

But shortly after he was delivered, he fell into a most serious illness and, staring death in the face, he thought that there was no hope for him. So again, what does the king do? I have no doubt that both he and the prophet again addressed themselves to prayer. What happened after they had prayed? He was again delivered. And then what followed this second

[19] 2 Kings 18:17.
[20] 2 Kings 18:27; 19:4, 15-19.

deliverance? He and the prophet gave thanks to God. Once again, prayer and praise.

What further took place? After this second deliverance, the king fell into ambition and pride. He openly vaunted all his jewels and treasures as if he had gained them by his own efforts. What followed this? The prophet pronounced stern judgment on his house, so that Hezekiah yet again was humbled. On account of that humbling of the king, Isaiah offered him a measure of comfort in that the judgment would not fall during his lifetime. So the king gave thanks and said, 'The word of the Lord is good; for there will be peace and rest in my days.'[21]

When we pay attention to the whole course of this king's life, we see that his experience was of a constant falling and rising, of prayer and then of praise. For as long we carry about with us these bodies of clay, as Job says,[22] and are bogged down with them, and as long as the dregs of iniquity remain in our souls, we shall be constantly subjected to falling, and then rising, not through our own efforts, but by the grace of God. It is this same divine grace which leads us first to pray and then to praise. Thus king Hezekiah prayed for strength in his battles and then praised God for his victories and deliverances.

A Christian's chief exercise

Now, take heed to this lesson and learn from a king what should be the Christian's spiritual exercise, on account of the

[21] 2 Kings 20:19.

[22] Job 13:12: 'Your memories may be copared vnto ashes *and* your bodies to bodies of claye.' (GenB.)

fleetingness of our earthly lives and that corruption which always encircles us, causing us to slide back (for our sanctification is but begun and perfect holiness is never attained in this life). Because we are all subject to daily troubles and in our lives there are constant struggles, should this not be our chief exercise: continual praying and praising of God? I mean prayer that God will strengthen us in our falls and trials, and praise for the victories he gives. Those who seek to emulate Hezekiah in this shall be blessed as he was. Even though the believer's life is a continuous battle, the Lord will always lift him up and strengthen and comfort him with his Spirit. Unhappy are those who neglect this exercise of prayer when they are brought low, for if they do not plead for strength then they are not worthy of being raised up again. There is not one of us who is not subject to this human condition; therefore, if we would have God raise us up when we are laid low, we must constantly engage in prayer. That is why I recommend to you all prayer and praising. So much, then, for the course of this king's life.

The first part of the king's song

Here we gain an insight into the great trouble, perplexity and agitated state of mind that the king was in, and how he reacted. In the ninth verse he tells us that the song was composed after he had recovered from his sickness. In the next verse he then records the circumstances when he was cast into this trouble and distress: 'in the cutting off of my days'[23] refers to the moment when Isaiah told him that he was

---

[23] Verse 10: 'I said in yᵉ cutting of of my daies, I shal go to yᵉ gates of the graue; I am depriued of the residue of my yeres' (GenB). ESV translates as, 'In the middle of my days I must depart …'

about to die. The instant the prophet told him that, he fell into this fear. Even though he was a godly and holy king, as well commended as any other king in the Scriptures, as soon as he heard pronounced the sentence of death, he trembled and was exceedingly afraid. Surely, it could not be otherwise, for death is a twisting and tearing apart of that which the Lord has fashioned to be held together as soul and body. If our human bodies had remained in perfect obedience as they were first created, soul and body would never have been so twisted; but on account of disobedience and the violating of God's command, sin entered bringing this violent struggle, leading to the death that is the result of sin; the apostle writes of this in Romans 6.

We need to examine this further, for there have been both ungodly persons, as well as some who were good people, who have sought to die. Yet none of these longed for death for itself, since it goes against nature to seek the termination of our lives. The ungodly who have tried to kill themselves were seeking a better state than they had in this life; usually their consciences were tormented and vexed by demonic powers and they persuaded themselves that they would be released from the misery of their souls if only they could escape from the prison of their bodies. But they were deceived. When living becomes hell in the here and now, that is only a first instalment of the full torment once a man departs from this life; so these wretched people have been tragically beguiled. On the other hand, there have been some good people who have longed to die because they yearn for a better life beyond the grave. If they had not believed that the afterlife would be far better, they would not have sought for death. Because they looked for that greater joy, they thought they would prefer the bitterness of death to their present unhappy state. I acknowledge that death for those who are Christians is now sanctified in the death of our Master and Saviour Christ Jesus (for 'blessed are the dead who die in the Lord'[24]). However, even though death itself is sanctified in Christ, we are not yet wholly sanctified, for if we were we would not experience terror, pain, or even grief over death. For seeing that in the best of us there is a remnant of corruption (would to God it were only a mere remnant, for it is so foul and substantial that it is a shame even to speak of it!), and it is this corruption that works on our consciences; and fear is caused when the conscience is accused, and the more that accusation continues the greater is the distress and even terror.

It is true that when fear is brought on by our consciences, where faith resides in the soul that fear is tempered, and the hope of heavenly joy yet to come causes that fear to be a holy awe. Indeed, the prospect of heaven transcends and devours the fear so that those looking on at the believer think they have no fear at all. Yet, I concede that even the believer knows something of fear and sorrow, even though they are governed by the blessed hope of heavenly joy. But what of those who do not have this hope? The fear and anguish of the unbeliever is so great that it is impossible to describe it. Terrible must it be for a man to stand before God in his righteous justice! No living creature can ever gaze upon him. Terrible, too, for that man to have all his past sins, in all their grotesque ugliness and guilt, brought before him. And for such a person to be left destitute of hope will not be the least part of their grief.

[24] Rev. 14:13.

Yet so many give ne'er a thought to any of this; they will not even leave their beds on the Lord's Day, though it would only cost them one hour to come and hear the word of God. What a strange and wretched madness in the human soul, that men never give hell a thought until hell entraps and captures them!

The way to escape the fear of death

So where are these considerations about the fear of death leading us? The less we indulge in corrupt living, the less will be our fear. What does that mean for our spiritual exercises of prayer and praise? Surely that if we would rid ourselves of the fear of death we should seek to rid ourselves of our corrupt deeds, and then our consciences will be clean and our testimony before others blameless. But as long as we are preoccupied with our love of this world and its baubles, we will never be without that lurking fear of death. Why? None who set their affections on earthly pleasures and riches can escape grief and pain when all these things are torn away from them. Therefore, should we not all travail to manage our heart's affections in such a way that we enjoy material things but only in so far as they serve our love for God, and so that we only love ourselves as we love our neighbours? Then, as often as he calls to us there will be no alien love in our hearts drawing us away from him.

All our towns and cities have an established law which forbids us taking with us certain goods which are useful here, but would serve no purpose in the foreign land we intend to visit. In our walk with God, there are also certain goods that we cannot take with us to the heavenly land to which we are travelling: I refer to the love of this world with all the cares it brings, and to the love and lusts of the flesh. For the Christian pilgrim these are 'goods' that are plainly forbidden by the king of that country, for the heart that is fully taken up with these shall not gain admittance there. There is but one command that rings out concerning such carnal 'goods': we must cleanse our hearts of them and seek only to carry with us those wares that agree with the holiness of that heavenly land.

Therefore, let us purge ourselves from all other loves and cleave only to God's love so that, loving him above all else, by his love we may also love our neighbour. If I am able to learn this one lesson out of all that I have tried to say, then I would consider my soul's travail very well blessed. I keep insisting on it in order that it may sink deeply into all your hearts. Yet in spite of all this, good King Hezekiah still feared as death stretched out its hand towards him, and to me this suggests that all Christians will experience some of that fear.

Continuing with the first part of the king's song, we move on to consider what he actually said in his agitated state of mind. He began by saying that he saw that he was on the threshold of death: 'I must depart; I am consigned to the gates of Sheol' (verse 10). It was as if he said, 'As soon as I heard the prophet say that I would die, at once I began to prepare myself for it. For if the prophet's pronouncements always come to pass, and if there is no way out for me even through God's mercy, then it is certain that I am going to die. For this I know, even though I am a king—indeed, a king of renown—I am nonetheless mortal and not exempt from the grave. Therefore I must prepare myself for death.' Hezekiah knew that even when he had prepared himself, his imminent departure remained unchanged.

Surely if you followed this king's example, you would be a thousand times more able to face daily living even though you may not be sick. But if you have an over-optimistic, rosy view of life and do not like to think about dying, assuming that for you death is still a long way off, I have to contradict you and so does the Spirit of God. The truth is that the more ready you are to die, the more ready are you to live. Anyone who denies that does not tell the truth, even if he happens to be the best of physicians. It therefore follows that when serious illness, that harbinger of death, begins to tug at a man's ears, the sick man should at once be warned to prepare himself for the worst; for, as I have just said, the more prepared he is to die, the more able is he to live. Even though Hezekiah was a king, he was well aware that he was a mortal man.

Turning to consider how he began his song, the king gave three reasons why his impending death grieved him so much. If you merely glance at these reasons, you might think they carry little weight. But if you look at them more closely you will discover in them an underlying meaning. The first reason for his grief was this: 'I am deprived of the residue of my years.'[25] At this time he was only thirty-eight or thirty-nine years of age, and so might have lived twice as long in the normal course of nature, as David says.[26] At first it might appear as if this was no great reason for such profound grief, but it

---

[25] The words quoted here are exactly as printed in the sermon's text. Unless an earlier editor has altered the quotation, Bruce seems to be paraphrasing the first clause of verse 10. GenB reads: 'I said in ye cutting of of my daies, I shal go to ye gates of the graue'; ESV translates as 'I said, In the middle of my days I must depart.'

[26] Psa. 90:10.

was not only the loss of years that was upsetting him so much as the loss of the opportunities which were being taken from him. Thus the more important reason for his sorrow was that the work of reformation that he had begun of both kirk and nation would now cease. Therefore this untimely cutting off of his days meant that he was not so well prepared to die as he might have been had he been granted more years to complete his task. It was not as if he was as unprepared for death as many younger men are who, assuming that they still have plenty of time, have postponed any intention to repent until they are much older. Rather was it that if he was to die just then the work of reformation would be unfinished. Hence this grief which caused him to say, 'I am deprived of the residue of my years.'

When we compare this to our own nation's cause I think that all of us must see clearly that unless we apply ourselves far more diligently to the work of reformation than we are apparently doing at present, I fear that we will not only leave this task unfinished but hardly started. For if the confusion in both kirk and state continues to increase each day, as it seems to be doing uninterrupted, as if there were no king in God's 'Israel', there is no doubt but that the outpouring of wickedness shall so increase in our land as to cause our people to be spewed out into the flood of filth. I am quite certain that there is no magistrate of any standing who is not lawfully forewarned of this and so rendered inexcusable before God. I leave that with you!

The second part of the king's song

The second reason why Hezekiah's imminent death grieved him so deeply is set down in verse 11: 'I said, I shall not see the Lord, the Lord in the land of the living.' What did he mean? I believe that he had the same desire to see the Lord that David had. What kind of desire is David referring to in Psalm 16 verse 8 where he says, 'I have set the Lord always before me'? He rejoiced greatly as he went on to say that his heart was glad, for he was sure that his soul would be gathered with his predecessors who were now in the presence of God where there is fullness of joy and sweetness of life for ever. I am convinced that this good man was not destitute of this vision, but in some measure he glimpsed it as his father David had done. So how is it that he can say here, 'I shall not see the Lord'? He goes on to explain what he means in the second part of the verse. It is as though he was saying, 'I shall not see him as I have seen him in past days, for I have seen him in his kirk, just as the rest of his faithful servants have seen him.'

You may ask what this means. Do you not know the teaching of the Scriptures in this matter? God was said to have been seen in ancient times when he was present in the visible symbols of his presence that he gave to his people. For the invisible God was said to have been seen in those symbols, first through the furnishings of the tent of meeting, and then later in the temple. God was said to be seen chiefly in the ark, for around it shone the divine presence, the cloud of his glory, which filled the Holy of Holies. Therefore, not seeing the Lord in the land of the living meant he would no longer be in God's service nor see him in his temple as he had done in times past.

Surely in all of this he was following in the footsteps of his saintly father David, as we read in so many Psalms which date from the times of his persecution. Nothing grieved David so deeply as being unable to join the throng of those who went to worship the Lord.[27] In Psalm 122 David begins, 'I was glad when they said to me, "Let us go to the house of the LORD!"' This singular, godly love for the word of God has been bequeathed to this king. That is why he is now grieving so deeply.

Now let us compare ourselves with Hezekiah and ask ourselves whether or not we follow him in this; that is, whether we have such a strong desire as he had to hear the word. Surely he will condemn every strata of our society. What of the great numbers of working folk of our country? What does their behaviour tell us about their hearing of the word? If they have some job to do it is put off until the Lord's Day; or if there needs to be a market or even a visit to someone in trouble, again it is delayed until the Sabbath Day. So what of the prosperous citizens of this town? Most have taken such a scunner at God's word that they cannot be bothered to rise early enough in the morning to come and hear it, even if the time were fixed at just one hour before your midday meal. Where will this contempt for the word lead us? It is bound to bring a famine of God's word in our land, for the Lord will not permit his word, so choice and so sweet, to be despised.

---

[27] Psa. 42:1-4; David also yearns for God's house in Psalms 55, 68, 84, *et al.* Calvin writes that Hezekiah valued the spiritual beholding of God granted to believers and, citing Psa. 42:2, continues: 'David says that they see the face of God who confirm their faith by the exercises of piety in the sanctuary.' *Comm. in loc.*

Yet it remains the same word which in the past your fathers and many of you have travelled long miles to hear; yet it is just as choice and sweet now as it was then. Unless there is a far greater zeal to hear it, it will be taken away from us by force. So much then for the second reason for the song.

The third part of the king's song

The third reason for his lament was, 'I shall look on man no more among the inhabitants of the world' [verse 11b]. This appears at first to be a very trivial reason for him to be grieved by the prospect of death. I am sure that there were some living at his time whom he took no pleasure in seeing, and who were to him a cause of sorrow; there are such monsters living among us today. But this statement rather refers to faithful men, honest and law-abiding both before their God and their king; they were his loyal subjects who lived under his protection and whose company gave him pleasure. It was these good men whom he would see no more. He had such a concern for the church of God, the believing citizens under him, that in the very hour of his death he could not hide his compassion for them, and he was grieved that they should no longer have his protection.

Consider how exceedingly blessed the realm is that has such a prince, who is imbued with the care of his subjects and especially of the kirk, that in his hour of death he laments that they should be deprived of his protection. By contrast, how cursed and miserable is the realm whose king has no care or concern for his people, least of all for the kirk of God whose faithful members are the most loyal of his subjects. Therefore, it is the duty of all of you who hear me today and who understand what it is to lack this blessing, to pray earnestly to God that he would distil his grace into his Majesty's heart, to pray to God that he will adopt a different attitude towards the protection of the kirk than he has shown until now. Would to God it were so! So much, then, for this brief exposition of the reasons for King Hezekiah's song.

What is worthy of praise, or of reproof, in these three reasons

In these three reasons for his song, some things (but not all them) are worthy of praise, for I do not find myself able to commend them all. Those are worthy of commendation that flowed from faith and were directed to the glory of God and the well-being of his kirk. But others are worthy of reproof insofar as they flowed from the foolish emotions and corruption of his fallen human nature. All of us, so long as we live in this world, have a share in the same effects of that fallen-ness; the only baggage of our earthly possessions that we carry with us on life's journey is this same corruption with its foolish desires. We cannot deny that kings have the authority to carry their jewels and wealth with them; but they also carry with them their vices and the errors they make in government, and such evil possessions will ultimately confront them. Surely if this good King Hezekiah carried such corrupt baggage with him, even more so will other kings. But it is the same for all of us; we all carry with us either virtues and vices. And if the main baggage we take with us on our pilgrimage to the heavenly city consists in the virtues of godliness, then when we arrive a clear and cleansed conscience will be there to greet us.

THE WAY TO TRUE PEACE AND REST

A concluding exhortation

Here is the sum of the matter that we have been considering: prepare yourselves first by emptying both your hands and your hearts of the love and desires of this world, and second ensure that your hearts are occupied only with the love of good things, so that when the Lord calls you may not be ashamed of the hearts you are carrying. And if your ears are inclined and open to receive this word, let it then be digested and incorporated into your souls, so that when you come to die the effects of your godly living may be plainly evident. And since we must carry with us either virtues or vices, that is, God's favour offering mercy, or else Satan's favour leading to judgment, should not our whole endeavour be that foul vices should be purged from our hearts? And should not all our striving be that our souls, which are prisoners in chains of wickedness, might be set at liberty and freedom from the pall of evil? Then we will have tender hearts as we acknowledge that by the blood of Christ our sins are forgiven; hearts whose anchorage of faith is in his blood, and whose sure hope is in his mercy; then we may have the seal of his peace which flows from our reconciliation purchased by the offering up of Christ's own body.

Now, when I see my own conscience at rest in his peace, and my soul so washed from the stains of corruption that all my sins are forgiven, am I not happy? But this can never be for you, unless in your hearts you are as attentive as you are just now in hearing me with your ears. But if this word, which is being heard by your ears, is digested and embedded in your hearts, then we would see right now much more progress in sanctification and newness of life than we presently do; and then death would not be nearly so daunting as it is to many of you. For the clear way of being rid of the fear of death is not to delay your repentance, but for repentance to be renewed every day of your lives.

How happy are those who have learned this lesson, and more than happy are those who live by it. But alas for those who never practise it! May the Lord so work within us, and grant us such increase of his Spirit, that we may follow it and study to practise it in all we do and say. The Lord God grant this may so by the righteous merits of Jesus Christ, to whom, with the Father and the Holy Spirit, be all praise, honour and glory, both now and for ever. Amen.

The Fourth Sermon

Upon Isaiah Chapter 38

My dwelling is plucked up and removed from me like a shep-
herd's tent; like a weaver I have rolled up my life; he cuts me
off from the loom; from day to night you bring me to an end;
[13] I calmed myself until morning; like a lion he breaks all my
bones; from day to night you bring me to an end. [14] Like a
swallow or a crane I chirp; I moan like a dove. My eyes are
weary with looking upward. O Lord, I am oppressed; be my
pledge of safety!—Isaiah 38:12-14

IN our last lesson, well-beloved in Christ Jesus, we saw how
by a wonderful sign the prophet assured the king of his full
recovery. The manner and form of the manifestation of the
sign were as follows: first, the king asked for a sign and the
Lord granted his request; second, Isaiah was the instrument
through whom his prayer was answered; third, the Lord gave
this sign by his own power and virtue[1] without the use of any
human agency. In seeking a sign, the king was not distrusting
God's promise, neither was he tempting God as the wicked

[1] On 'virtue' see The Third Sermon, Note 16.

do; rather he sought to affirm his faith in God's word. Though his faith was weak, nonetheless he believed the promise.

You ask, 'Why was his faith weak?' Within the space of less than an hour, Isaiah had brought to him two completely opposing pronouncements. The first was to tell him to set his house in order, for he was soon to die; then just a little later he told him, 'You are going to live for fifteen years!' But both of these messages could not stand. That was why the king asked for a sign—he needed assurance that the promise of his recovery was true. So it was that the sun moved back and the shadow on his father's horologe also moved back by ten degrees. We saw that a day that ought to have lasted for twelve hours in fact lasted for twenty-four hours. The sign was confirmed both in the sun's movement and in the shadow on the horologe. We guess that as Ahaz's dial was set up in a public place in front of the royal residence close to the temple, therefore the sign would have been seen and known about throughout the city, and news of it would have travelled throughout Judea. Moreover, because the sign was evident in the sun's backward movement, the whole world must have witnessed a miracle wrought by God the like of which had never been seen before.

We see, therefore, that the sign was clear and fit for its purpose. The king now saw clearly that it was as easy for God to bring back his life to its original youthful bloom, though it had been slipping away, as it was for God to bring the sun back ten hours even though it had been approaching sunset. Only by the power of God could this have happened, for it is an inviolable principle that no human being, not even the devil himself, is able to work a genuine miracle. The supposed miracles in some Roman Catholic churches, such as those worked by relics, are deceptions of the devil. Hezekiah was granted this sign simply in response to his prayer in order to teach us this lesson: if it is the Lord's will and purpose to bestow on us some benefit, and even if that benefit has been promised, he only gives to those who earnestly seek. God would have us to seek him before we obtain the good things he has for us. So he would have us learn this lesson that we might always honour and worship him who has benefits to give us.

Before we began to think about the king's song, I brought before you a bird's-eye view of the fourteen years of his reign,[2] and we noted that during those years there was in his life a constant falling and rising, praying and praising: praying in his troubles that the Lord would strengthen him by his Spirit; praising him in the hour of victory that the Lord had so mightily delivered him. Herein we see a picture of the Christian life and exercise, to assure each of us that as long as we are here on earth our lives will follow the same pattern of falling and rising—that is, rising by the special grace and mercy of God in Christ Jesus. And therefore it behoves you all to engage in the same exercises that this king engaged in: when you enter the trough of troubles to be diligent in prayer, seeking the Lord's strength to endure; and then praising him in your victories. The one who forgets to pray also forgets to rise. So take heed that in all your trials you always have recourse to God in prayer.

• Let me remind you also of what we have seen regarding Hezekiah's song. It is in three parts, in the first of which he

[2] 2 Kings 18:13.

sets down the great troubles and distress that he was in, and what he said and did at that time. In the second part he gives an account of how remarkable and excellent the great blessing was that he received. In the third part he made a faithful promise to be ever thankful to God for his favour: he would praise him every day, and so long as he lived he would never forget him.

In the first part we noted at what point this great distress overwhelmed him, namely, when it was that God's servant came to him and told him he was going to die. The moment he received that news, the prospect of his imminent death filled him with fear and trembling; it threw him into the greatest distress. Even though he was a godly king, indeed, such a king of whom there is made as much favourable commendation as there is of any other ruler in the Holy Scriptures; nevertheless, at the pronouncement that he was about to die, he was greatly afraid. Why should this have been? It was because death is always a tearing asunder of two parts of our lives that ought always to be held together. Therefore we should not be surprised that the prospect of it strikes fear into the human heart. Death is the result of our own sin and in some ways it is good that we should be given a taste of what sin has brought upon us.

On the one hand, it is undoubtedly true that for those who are Christians death has been fully sanctified in the death of Christ Jesus. But on the other hand, even though the believer's death is fully sanctified, yet so long as there remains, even in the best of us, a remnant of corruption—and would to God it were only a remnant!—from it there flows this fear and distress. It is true that faith and the constant hope of a better life to come are rooted in that other part of the believer's soul, and these do temper the fear, mitigate the trouble, and swallow up the pain of death. Yet on account of that remnant of corruption some fear will creep in, and the greater the remaining corruption in a man's soul, the greater is the fear that strikes the conscience.

The chief grief of our corruption that grieves us at the approach of death is the love of this world, its cares, and our infatuation with flesh and blood; therefore those who would rid themselves of the fear of death must first rid themselves of such inordinate worldly affections. From sad experience we learn that none who are entwined in some such love can avoid exceeding grief. For in the article of death is writ large the cost of affections set on frivolous things that one day will suddenly evaporate. So I repeat yet again that now is the time to rid your hands and purge your hearts of all preposterous affections, so that death—to so many a terrible prospect—when it comes will be to you a blessing.

I have already explained to you that these worldly cares are forbidden baggage expressly prohibited by the king of heaven; they are neither profitable to you nor admissible to the country where you are going. That is why I have urged you to take on your journey the love of God and his love in you for your neighbour. Such wares will both profit you and be welcome in that heavenly land to which you are travelling.

Back to the king. In his trouble the first thing he uttered, speaking with himself was, 'In the middle of my days I must depart; I am consigned to the gates of the grave.' Even though he was loath to die, as his words indicate, he began to ready himself. It is foolish and false to think that preparing for death is aiding and abetting death. No, the very opposite! The more ready you are to die, the more able are you to live, and the less shall be your anguish when the Lord calls you. As far as this good King Hezekiah was concerned, the only reasons that I will mention for his distress over the prospect of death were first the great love he had for the kirk in his country, and second the deep concern he had for his faithful subjects who would be losing his merciful protection by his death. How exceedingly blessed was his realm when he was so concerned for the kirk and for his people that on the threshold of the grave it was them he thought of and was grieved to be leaving. By contrast, how heavily cursed is the realm in which its prince has neither care for the kirk nor concern for his faithful subjects!

Regarding other reasons that cause believers distress in facing death, I would not justify them all. I believe that the word of God tells us that some are worthy of commendation, but others deserve reproof. So far as they arise from faith and from the Spirit of God, they are worthy of praise, but in so far as they arise from unruly affections they deserve censure. In the king's case, it would appear from the words of his song that not all of his affections were praiseworthy. So the lesson we learned was that the harvest we reap from our stupid affections is that they transfer our love from God the Creator to the creatures he has made; and before our love can be wrested from those creatures, they cause us such an intense grief that it is like another death. Therefore the plea that I brought to you was that you should set your affections upon God. True love resides in God, and so it becomes you to transfer your hearts' affections from created things and to give them to

God in whom only is lasting and real joy. This is as far as we proceeded in my last address to you.

Our text for today

> My dwelling is plucked up and removed from me like a shepherd's tent; like a weaver I have rolled up my life; he cuts me off from the loom; from day to night you bring me to an end; [13] I calmed myself until morning; like a lion he breaks all my bones; from day to night you bring me to an end. [14] Like a swallow or a crane I chirp; I moan like a dove. My eyes are weary with looking upward. O Lord, I am oppressed; be my pledge of safety!

In these verses that I read this morning the king returns to his complaint and lamentation. In the first part of verse 12 he writes of the trouble he was in. Then in the second part of that verse and on into verse 13 the heat and fury of his raging illness cause him to groan in its pangs. In verse 14 he gives us an insight into how he reacted in the extremities to which his sickness had driven him. So let us begin with the twelfth verse and his lamentation.

He continues with his complaint of verses 10 and 11, bursting out in the words, 'My dwelling is plucked up and removed from me.' He is in effect saying, 'My life here is about to end, and the Lord is transporting it to another place; I see that death is close, and the Lord is cutting off my time on earth.' He uses two similes: the first is of a shepherd's tent and the second is of a weaver and his loom.

The first similitude: the shepherd's tent

See how a shepherd's tent is dismantled, loaded on to a cart and taken away somewhere else; like that, writes the king, is my life being removed to some other place. Those of you who read histories will already know that in the East and other hot countries, for example among the Arabs and Tartars, shepherds use tents during the summer, and whenever they move their flocks on, they take their tents with them. In the same way here in Scotland whenever shepherds move on their flocks to fresh pasture, they also move their hurdles,[3] just as eastern shepherds move their tents. So the king says, 'See how the shepherds' tents are moved from one place to another during the summer; that is what is happening to my life.'

This similitude is a parable containing sound teaching for us. First, we learn that there is nothing more unstable than human life here on earth; as long as we are in these bodies our lives are subject to uncertainty. The human body is like a tent, but tents were never intended to be fixed dwellings; they have no foundations as houses do, but are simply held down by wooden pins in the ground. In a strong wind they shake and if the pins are loosened the tents can collapse. So the king's illustration is teaching us that these lives of ours have no permanent feu,[4] no firm foundation, and therefore no security. Therefore the king would direct our minds to another life which has freehold, solid foundations, and complete security; he is pointing us to that other kingdom of which the apostle writes in Hebrews 12:28 that cannot be shaken.[5] If my mem-

---

[3] Bruce's phrase is 'flit their flaikis'. A 'flaik' was a 'hurdle', that is, 'a portable framework made of crossed wattles or thin willow branches'; 'flaik' can also mean 'a plaid', which was placed over the hurdle for protection from bad weather.

[4] The Scots word 'feu' is derived from 'feudal' and means 'a land tenure for which a small annual payment is made'.

[5] Heb. 12:28: 'Wherefore seing that we receiue a kingdome, which can

ory serves me correctly in the previous chapter, at verses 9 and 10, the apostle sketches a picture[6] that contrasts the shepherd's tent and the city of God;[7] he is saying that as the tents lack any foundation and feu, by contrast the city of God had a permanent tenure and foundation. However, he does not use the singular but the plural for 'foundations';[8] 'Look,' he says, 'to the city that has foundations, whose craftsman and builder is the God of heaven.' And it is in the words to which I have just referred in chapter 12 where he says such a kingdom cannot be shaken, that he explains what he means: the ground of this city's tenure is so secure that no passage of time or stormy blasts can shake it or make it flounder. The first benefit[9] you have from this city of God (contrasted with a mere tent) is this: learn to strive for this city that has foundations; seek for the city that cannot be shaken. The Lord give you grace!

There is another aspect of this comparison. It is that the apostle lets us see that so long as we are in this life we have no

---

not be shaken, let vs haue grace, whereby we may so serue God, that we may please him with reuerēce and feare' (Gen.B).

[6] Bruce's phrase is 'a plat contrast'; 'plat' can mean a 'diagram' or 'map' or 'a plan of a piece of territory'.

[7] Heb. 11:9-10: 'By faith he abode in the land of promes, as in a strange countrey, as one that dwelt in tentes with Isaac and Iacob heirs with him of the same promes. For he loked for a citie hauing a fundacion, whose buylder and maker is God' (GenB).

[8] Interestingly, though we know Bruce used the Geneva Bible which has the singular 'fundacion' (his copy is still in the possession of his family), he must have been working from either a Greek Testament which has the plural *themelious* or a Latin Bible which had the plural *fundamenta*.

[9] The word Bruce uses is 'commoditie' which in the Braid Scots meant 'the advantages or benefits derived from the use or possession of some landed property'.

permanent lodging nor certainty of being sure how long we can continue staying here. For as you may perceive from the accounts in Genesis, the patriarchs lived in tents in order to bear witness to two points. First, they testify to us that they were neither citizens nor natives of that land, but aliens and pilgrims there; they themselves acknowledged that they were strangers in the land so long as they remained here on earth.[10] The second thing to which they bore witness by living in tents was that they had no intention of remaining there; it was not their plan to put down their stakes, as we say, for they were on a journey, seeking the way that would lead them homeward, the path to their true native country, to this city that has foundations, as they themselves confessed.

Then there is yet another benefit[11] that we may reap from this similitude. It teaches us that because we have no certain or permanent dwelling here, we ought not to set our hearts or our love on anything here.[12] Seeing that all of us are sub-

---

[10] There are many allusions to this, both direct and indirect: Gen. 15:7-8; 23:4; 24:3-4, *et al.*

[11] See note 9 above.

[12] Bruce knew from experience the reality of what he is urging. Regarding the total turnabout in his life when he left his profession as an advocate and member of the elite Court of Session and went to St Andrews to study for the ministry, he wrote: 'It was long before I could get leave to go. My mother made me such an impediment. My father at last consented, but my mother would not, till I had denuded my hands of some lands and casualities I was infeft in.' D.C. MacNicol, *Robert Bruce, Minister in the Kirk of Edinburgh* (London: Banner of Truth Trust, 1961) p. 28. A 'casuality' was income paid to a landlord; 'infeft' means that he owned investments of heritable property (his father had given him the estate of Kinnaird, Larbert); therefore he is saying that he denuded himself of a considerable income which was his by hereditary right.

ject to that final flitting and know not the day or hour, be assured that there is nothing more certain than our departure from this life nor anything more unknown than when that will be. Therefore, it behoves us now while we still have the opportunity to pack up all our possessions and to send them ahead of us to our permanent dwelling-place, yes, to invest our substance where we are to live for ever. Surely you all know from experience that even though you may be fit and well, it is quite certain that one day you will have to flit. That being so, will you not lay up your treasure in heaven? Seeing therefore you all know in your hearts that none of you can live on and on here indefinitely, and that none of you know when the summons to depart will come, it is obvious that we must prepare ourselves by sending on ahead of us all of our substance, all of our wealth. And since our Master says that where our treasure is, there will our hearts be also, let both heart and treasure be invested in heaven.

Surely this is a most singular benefit, the knowledge of which we must learn well. For a man must be out of his mind to invest his future happiness in a place where he cannot remain and where he has no idea when he will be called on to depart. I am quite sure that everyone here will agree with me. Nonetheless, I am equally sure that all of you here continue to please yourselves. Therefore there is something of which I must remind you: I refer you to the parable recorded in Luke 12 where we are told of a rich man who pulled down his barns and built greater ones to store his ever-increasing harvest; he then said to himself, 'Take your rest, eat, drink and enjoy yourself.' This insatiable fool, as our Master called him, did not realize that his summons to depart had already been issued and would shortly be given to him. But had he been aware that only limited times and seasons belonged to him, he would not have made those plans for himself. For we see in the parable how his grand scheme came to nothing and his hopes were dashed, when that very night everything was taken from him.

Now I know that none of you are so stupid that you would take on your lips the same words as this rich man. Nevertheless, I also know that you are foolish enough to do exactly what he did because in your hearts that is what you are planning. Always, I say, such motives are false and proceed from dim-witted brains. The worldly wisdom that induces men to think like that is plain folly and can only bring disappointment. The only safe resolution for you to make is one that flows from the truth of God's word, for that is sure and steadfast. Therefore, all of you, make certain that your warrants for living are based on his truth.

The Scriptures say that none of us have any certainty of tomorrow, not even for one more hour of our lives. So this parable admonishes us all to be prepared. And if you desire riches, seeing that riches are the Lord's inheritance bequeathed to you, store up the riches of godly living so that you can invest in heaven those eternal goods that are welcome there. Be rich in God and then in eternity you and riches will never be parted. If we only learn this one lesson this morning, then this day's exercise will have been employed well. In short, let all of you so resolve that when the messenger of death comes to you, whenever that might be, you will be prepared. So much for this first similitude of the shepherd's tent.

The second similitude: the weaver's loom

In the second part of verse 12 he says in effect, 'I have been doing my work, weaving at the loom of my life to the end of the cloth. My life is now woven, the fragile material I have made is going to be cut off from the loom.'[13] He means that the uncompleted cloth has become an off-cut, his days have been prematurely shortened; he himself has somehow become responsible for his untimely death. He is telling us that he has hastened the day of his departure, because by the evil he has done he has shortened his life. Certainly it is true that as by sin death entered the world, so by multiplying our sins we hasten our deaths. Human mortality is no accident; it is the consequence of human sin. It is possible for sin to be the cause of an early death. As Jacob said when Pharaoh asked him how many were the days of the years of life, 'Few and evil have been the days of the years of my life.'[14] Sin can fill our days with anguish and grief, trouble and sorrow; sin entwines us in a thousand cares and in exceedingly deceitful vanities. Sin can consume us with unprofitable labours and unnecessary travails. What more? Sin weakens our mortal bodies by deceptive pleasures; it is able to vex our minds with such fears that are too dreadful to put into words. In short, everything that causes God to turn away his face flows from sin.

If it was true that this fine king had genuine cause to say that it was his sin that hastened his death, if so godly a king

[13] Bruce's word here, which I have translated as 'fragile material', is 'web' which refers to 'a coarse, thin, white sarge, stearched, and often rent in stearching by a violent exertion of the manufacturer, who soon lost a lucrative trade by indulging an intemperate thirst of gain'. (*Dictionar o the Scots Leid*, http://www.dsl.ac.uk/dsl)

[14] Gen. 47:9.

who had been so good when he was a youth could declare that sin had shortened his days, what then may the youth of our nation say? I pray you, what may our young nobility say? Surely if this king lived in such a way as almost brought him to a premature death, what shall we say of those who have walked even faster along this way, even competing to run the fastest towards some evil scheme—unless God himself intervene? The Psalmist writes that 'men of blood and treachery shall not live out half their days'.[15] If this be true, what shall become of the bloody adulterer,[16] or of the sacrilegious blasphemer, or of the idolatrous priest and those of a host of other vices—all of whom hurry fast along this same road? If the allotted span of someone with only one single vice shall be cut short, how much more shall the years be shortened of those in whose lives many vices conspire together? It cannot fail to happen. But let us turn from the powerful and wealthy.

Consider the ordinary working folk: anyone can see that they too hurry along this same pathway. There are two sins which are common to them: gluttony and drunkenness. And we all know that these two excesses cause all kinds of physical illnesses; but the chief illness they cause is sickness of the soul and that will cause them to perish for ever. In Proverbs 23 Solomon asks, 'With whom lodges fear, sorrow, contention, debate and strife? With whom but with him who loves wine?'[17] And yet see how the majority of people in the towns

[15] Psa. 55:23.

[16] Bruce here is most likely referring to the 'spiritual adultery' of those whose infidelity was to the truth of the Scriptures and who were shedding the blood of the Lord's people.

[17] Bruce is evidently quoting from memory. In his Bible Prov. 23:29-30

and villages of our country are seeking to spend what little they have in order to indulge in such evils. It is a terrible thing to fall into the hands of God,[18] and yet all who abandon themselves to such vices will fall into his hands. For it cannot be but that the wrath of God from heaven must be poured out upon such ungodliness. And there is none who has given over his soul and body to such vices who shall not perish in his sin, unless he be saved by some miraculous intervention. There are worse sins than this that incur the judgment of God. For example, we read in John 8 that Jesus warned the Pharisees that they would die in their sins;[19] that was counted a most terrible judgment.

Is the word now being proclaimed able to summon men back from their sins? Indeed so, and surely it has been sounded forth clearly and constantly; but when I consider its effects, it is apparent that the effect of the preaching of this word on most of my hearers has been to harden their hearts and so to seal up their judgment against the day of the Lord's wrath. That final day of reckoning they have deliberately forgotten about and scrubbed from their minds, lest they should think about it again. O that the Lord by his Spirit would instil this light into us, so that by it we may see that there is a heaven and a hell, and that, perceiving the danger, we may

---

reads: 'To whome is wo? to whome is sorowe? to whome is strife? to whome is murmuring? to whome are woundes without cause? ... Euan to them that tarie long at the wine, to them that go, and seke mixt wine' (GenB).

[18] Heb. 10:31: 'It is a feareful thing to fall into the hands of the liuing God' (GenB).

[19] John 8:24: 'I said therefore vnto you, That ye shall dye in your sinnes: for except ye beleue, that I am he, ye shall dye in your sinnes' (GenB).

resolve to avoid it, and, seeing the felicity, may determine to embrace it. Would to God that it were so!

Hezekiah goes on to say, 'He cuts me off from the loom.' He means the 'throombs that go about the beam'.[20] He is saying that just as the weaver cuts off that fragile material[21] from the throombs of his beam, so the Lord has purposely resolved to cut off his life from his loom. Notice the counteraction between the two persons involved, for the king is letting us glimpse the understanding and knowledge he has of himself: he attributes the 'cutting off' to God, but he acknowledges the cause lies with himself. Likewise he attributes the chastisement to God, but it is all his fault because his sin is the reason for the chastisement. God has his part in what has been happening, but he, the king, also has his part in it. God has initiated it, just as he does in everything that happens. All that flows from human nature is warped, but all that flows from God is holy and just. How wise of Hezekiah to acknowledge that the cause of God's severity towards him lay entirely with himself! Happy are those who admit their sin and are honest about their guilt; such persons will not fall under the condemnation of God.

The pain of a troubled soul and a guilty conscience

We come now to the last part of verse 12 and to all of verse 13.

… from day to night you bring me to an end; [13] I calmed myself until morning; like a lion he breaks all my bones; from day to night you bring me to an end.

[20] I am using Bruce's actual phrase; 'throombs that go about the beam' were unwoven ends of the warp-threads left attached to the loom (beam); such threads were used in making other articles.

[21] See Note 13 above.

Hezekiah now tells us how severe was the disease that racked his body. It was a high fever that raged throughout his whole body. In these verses he speaks of the intensity of the illness and in effect says this: 'If God continues with me as he has started, before the evening comes he will finish me off by means of this fever.' And in verse 13 he says, 'I placed this all before myself, and waited expectantly for it to happen: that like a devouring lion he should bruise all my bones.' I take it that all this occurred within twenty-four hours.

But there is much more in these words than a reference to his physical pain, for it is not possible that so good a king could have spoken like this about God unless he had been suffering from something more than a bodily illness. So in uttering these words he is letting us see something of his anguished soul and troubled conscience—these join themselves with the pain of his diseased body. That is why he felt that God was manifesting himself as a consuming fire. He could never have likened God to a devouring lion unless there was an altogether different fever, as well as the fever of his body. Remember David's words when he also was in an extremity of body and soul: 'My bones are vexed and my soul is greatly troubled.'[22]

Of all the various illnesses that can befall any person, there cannot be any doubt that the greatest illness is the sickness of the soul and conscience. And of all the spiritual troubles that can overtake the conscience, without question this is the greatest: when with the sight of our sin—which is more than a soul can bear—joined to it is an awareness of the wrath of

[22] Psa. 6:2b-3a, 'o Lord heale me, for my bones are vexed. My soule also is sore troubled ...' (GenB).

God. Oh! then this sickness becomes unbearable! Merciful God! when the horror is exceedingly great and terrible, is it not astonishing that the soul can stand firm on your promises, and yet be unrestrained in its spiritual desperation! Nevertheless, it is true that every notable servant of God has had this experience, some in greater intensity than others; each one has been touched with the terror of the hell which the reprobate shall have in full measure.

Why God allows his dear ones to suffer

There is a reason why the Lord allows his children to endure such extremities as did the king. His purpose is for them to see clearly what Christ has suffered as he bore the full weight of his Father's wrath inflamed against our sins; not only against the sins of those who are afflicted, but his wrath against the sins of all his elect children. He casts them into such extremities so that they will realize that as a result of Christ's suffering for them they are now under obligation to their Lord; also, so that they will understand a little of how precious that redemption, purchased by his blood, should be to us all. No one can understand the value of a benefit unless he is aware that it is genuinely a benefit; by the same token, you cannot truly value heaven unless you have had a taste of hell. He sends his servants along the road to heaven because he would have them pass close by the gates of hell: then they will clearly see that there was no collusion[23] between the Father and the Son, as

---

[23] By 'collusion' Bruce means a secret pact between the Father and the Son. It is uncertain to what Bruce is referring. It may have been to the Docetae who denied the reality of Christ's body and therefore denied the reality of his death. (Cunningham, *Historical Theology*, vol. 1, [1862; repr. London: Banner of Truth Trust, 1960], p. 124.)

some wicked persons have suggested. Therefore, I repeat that God permits his servants to taste the suffering of hell so that they can truly say, 'I understand just a little of the anguish of Christ who endured sin's penalty that he might redeem us from hell.'[24] Although none such as you and me are able to endure such anguish, even though we are only subjected to the merest taste of it, our Saviour has borne the full force of the anguish of God's wrath as he took upon himself the sins of all the elect. In this way God lets his dear ones understand how great a debt of gratitude we owe to him.

The dissolute living of the godless multitude lets us see clearly that not one of them has ever taken to heart this sacred message. (For many of you it is still an unopened letter whose seal has never been broken!) This is why they take no account of the death of Christ, and just assume that it was his own fault. It appears that they have no sense of sin, far less remorse, yet it is their sin that will destroy them—as their manifest contempt for the things of God make clear—unless there can be some intervention; the more they are bidden, the more they pursue all kinds of sin.

In Hebrews 10 the apostle is more outspoken and pointed than many other biblical writers in his warnings against such behaviour: 'Anyone who has set aside the law of Moses dies without mercy on the evidence of two or three witnesses. How

---

[24] It could well be that Bruce is following Calvin here. On the simile of the lion, Calvin writes: 'Besides, there is no cruelty and fierceness in wild beasts that is fitted to strike such terror as we feel from the bare mention of the name of God, and justly; for the Lord's chastisements must have sufficient power to humble and cast us down to hell itself, so that we shall be almost destitute of consolation and regard everything as full of horror.' (*Comm. in loc.*)

much worse punishment, do you think, will be deserved by the one who has spurned the Son of God, and has profaned the blood of the covenant by which he was sanctified, and has outraged the Spirit of grace?'[25] Even if these dire warnings do not take effect immediately (the Lord's promises likewise are not always fulfilled quickly), and even if you do not believe them, yet I must still declare them, that these walls may testify and bear witness to your consciences that there was a prophet among you, and so that one day you will have to admit, 'All this was told us and we were given opportunity to respond, if only we had taken heed.'

Before we proceed to the next verse, I want to say that there are in Scripture a few other incidents similar to Hezekiah's experience, concerning both men and women. It is important that we take note of them for they teach us this same lesson of God acting to subdue the pride of the flesh. It is easy for the Lord to defy the stupidity and depravity of youth in a very short time; why, in the space of only twelve hours an excellent king was brought to the very gates of death. Therefore you should say to yourselves, 'It is time to change our course, for now we see how easy it is for the Lord to lay low those lifted up with foolish vanity.' When the Lord brought Hezekiah low he did not need fire or sword or a suit of armour, nor did he use some hitherto unheard-of device. He simply used the king's physical body, his frail flesh in which he was conceived and born, for in that flesh resides that sin which is the reason for all God's chastening and plagues; yes, sin is the cause of death, both of body and soul. Thus there is within each of us a kind of store-house of the material

[25] Heb. 10:28-29.

the Lord uses when he chooses to afflict the best of those who foolishly think they can ignore his word. Therefore if you have the benefit of good health, learn to use it well, for if you abuse and defile your bodies which the Lord intends to be the temple of his Holy Spirit, just remember how easy it was for him to bring low a good king; consider how much easier it will be for him to bring low even the best of you. So I say to those who have good health, resolve to employ it for the honour and strengthening of his kirk, for he it is who has given you that good health.

In his pain Hezekiah sought the Lord

In the third part of today's text the king tells us what he did in his extremity and how he reacted in the burning pain of his sickness.

> Like a swallow or a crane I chirp; I moan like a dove. My eyes are weary with looking upward. O Lord, I am oppressed; be my pledge of safety!

We can see in this fourteenth verse that although he knew it was the Lord who was afflicting him, nonetheless he turned to him in that affliction, and sought to forge a new intimacy with the one who thus threatened him with death. We read that he sought the Lord in three ways. First, by speaking to him. As long as his body, so sorely stricken by the pain of his sickness, had strength enough to pray, he reached out to God with his lips. Second, when the disease robbed him of the ability to speak, he continued to seek God by silent mourning, moaning 'like a dove' and with deep lamentation 'like a swallow or a crane'. Third, in his gesture of lifting up his eyes to heaven until he was weary with watching.

So long as he was able to speak, the words he used were few but they were full of meaning: 'I am oppressed. Refresh me'; or 'I am oppressed, finish your work on the tapestry of my short life.' He is continuing in the simile in verse 12b of the weaver cutting off the 'throombs that go about the beam'.[26] It is as if he was saying, 'I can see that the raging fury of my sickness is so great that neither my body's natural resources nor human medicaments are able to relieve my pain and heal me; therefore seeing that there are no natural means of help I have no other recourse than to turn to the God who created nature, since it is easy for him to heal me when nature can offer no hope. So I beseech the Omnipotent God to weave out the rest of the web of my life, and to restore me to full health, for his glory and for the good of his kirk.' This I think is the meaning and substance of his prayer, whether he moaned or mourned, whether he spoke or wept.

Consider something further concerning his prayer. Does it not appear strange that Hezekiah should seek for the prolongation of his life, as if there was no better life after this, or another 'day' after this? But when we weigh up the facts and trace the course of his life, we find there were many reasons that caused him to pray as he did. We know that Manasseh his son had not been born[27] and that as yet he had no children, on whom he might see the pledges of God's favour and the fulfilment of the promises that had been made both to him and to his father's house, and not least of that promise concerning the Messiah. Now, having no heirs in whom he wanted to see the accomplishment of these promises, did he

---

[26] See note 20 above.
[27] 2 Kings 21:1.

not have good reason to seek the lengthening of his days until he should see God's word coming to fruition?

Briefly (I have already touched on this), in certain circumstances it is permissible to crave from God the prolongation of our lives. When it is for the benefit of the Lord's work, certain servants of God have asked for this. An example can be found in Philippians where the apostle counts it as a divine mercy both for himself and for Epaphroditus, his fellow worker and fellow soldier, who had been 'near to death', that he had been restored.[28] Therefore we too should likewise consider such restoration as a special mercy. Anyone who is absolutely certain in his mind that the lengthening of his days would be for the glory of God and the strengthening of his kirk, may in faith legitimately crave it. Nevertheless, there is a general condition to be borne in mind, as in all of our prayers, that we submit our wills and desires to be ruled by the good will of God in such a way that we are always ready to lay our lives and our possessions at his feet, and are always prepared to offer everything to him as a sacrifice when it so pleases him to ask this of us.

The first lesson from these three verses

The first thing I ask you to notice is the opposing moods reflected in the king's words in verses 13 and 14. Read them again to see this. In the second part of the thirteenth verse his voice is full of doubting,[29] even fear; he speaks as if God

---

[28] Phil. 2:25-30.

[29] I have retained Bruce's word 'doubting' (Old Scots 'dowtyng'), though its meaning is slightly different to that as used in twenty-first-century English. For Bruce 'doubting' included 'apprehension' and

was his deadly enemy. By contrast, in the fourteenth verse he appears to contradict himself, turning in prayer to the same God whom he has just spoken of as if he was his foe; but now he asks for his blessing, indicating that he trusts in this God. None can invoke him unless they trust him. So these are his reactions while suffering the dire illness. At one point he regards God as a consuming fire; but then he has recourse to him as his only refuge. One moment his speech is full of doubting, the next moment his words indicate he is full of confidence.

The question thus arises whether it is possible for both faith and doubting to have a place in one man's soul. I answer that is very possible and that every one of God's servants have experience of this. Be assured of this: there is no conscience so completely at rest that it is without any trouble, and there is no man so pure that his life is free of every iniquity. Therefore there are times when God chooses to bring his dearest children into this valley of doubting; nevertheless, when he does that he also sustains and protects them from despair. Do you not know that this faith of ours is never perfect, but is subject to continual development and growth, yet never in this life reaches total perfection? As long as we are here on earth we are subject to faltering,[30] to wrestling, to doubting, and to manifold errors. Yet all these imperfections are freely pardoned through the righteous merits of Jesus Christ. Where is the one who, if he places his soul under the spotlight of the

---

'fearing'. A little later in this sermon he equates it with affliction and perplexity (paraphrasing the latter as 'in doubt'), from 2 Cor. 4:8.

[30] Bruce's word is 'stammerings' which in his day meant both 'hesitations' and 'doubts'.

absolute perfection that is the nature of God—to whom only that which is perfect is pleasing—will not fall into dismay as soon as he beholds him?

So let a man examine his faith and compare it with the perfection demanded in the Scriptures and with that growth in grace exhorted on us, and is there any one who shall not fear? Let this personal examination be in the light of all that is craved of us in the holy writings, and so let that man cast his eyes on the manifold corruptions within, and let him also consider the heavy judgment of God hanging over the sinner's soul and body. Will he not then tremble? It is inevitable that he will as often as he searches his own heart and sees his unclean affections. So I say, this apprehension and doubting are the common experience of all the Lord's best servants.

I am sure that none of you will consider the apostle Paul to have been one of the worst of God's servants, yet his words make clear that he too had this doubting in his soul. In 2 Corinthians 4 verse 8 he says plainly, 'We are always in affliction, but not in distress; we are in doubt, but we despair not.'[31] So Paul admits that even in the soul that has faith there is a doubting, but he denies that it leads to despair. It is as if he is saying, 'I want you to understand that both doubting and faith may stand side by side in the Lord's servant, but not despair.' The reason he says this is that the whole concept of despair implies knocking down the very pillars of our beliefs; thus faith and despair are incompatible, whereas faith and doubting may both be lodging in my soul, and shall continue to lodge in the souls of all faithful believers until the end of this world. Under this word 'doubting' Paul includes all the

[31] See note 29 above.

errors, troubles, falterings and wrestlings, with which our faith is often assaulted, and which can one moment incline us to despair if we take our eyes off the Lord and the next to hope when we look upon the mercy of God in Christ Jesus. So we see that Paul considers this fear and apprehension (this 'doubting') as the experience of all Christians, including himself.

Some of you do take heed to this, knowing that you too may well be visited by God in the same way as he visited the king. Therefore, even though you do not experience this affliction yourselves, keep it in mind when you call on someone who is similarly visited by the Lord. Because the Spirit of faith and sanctification never completely finishes his work during our earthly lives, and a major part of these bodies of sin continue to be defiled with the remnants of corruption, we are at times bound to fall into faltering and fearing. And when that occurs in our lives, as it is bound to do, what such errors and troubles produce in us is nothing but sin. And if such sin is allowed to multiply, the result will be a cloud or a mist between us and our God. That is why the prophet called sin a 'partition' whereby we are deprived of the sight of God given to us in our Mediator.[32]

But suppose we do not succumb to some gross iniquity, yet still sin and its guilt fill us with apprehension and faltering, so clouding our vision and the eye of faith; there can be no doubt that then our resolve will be weakened and we will not be as steadfast in our Christian convictions as we were before.

---

[32] Perhaps an allusion to Isa. 59:2: 'Your iniquities have made a separation between you and your God, and your sins have hidden his face from you so that he does not hear.'

For those whose sight is dimmed will mistake one thing for something else. Thus this 'doubting' is always a consequence of our inner corruption, the vestiges of which in this life ever remain in our souls.

The second lesson from these three verses

The second lesson for us is that there is comfort and consolation here when we learn that it is common to all God's servants to be caught between two contrary emotions when in great trouble. One moment they will experience a deep sense of the love and mercy of God; the next moment they will sense his wrath and displeasure as if he were their deadly opponent. That is how it was with Hezekiah: at times his words expressed his fears and doubts, yet at other times he turned to God seeking his blessing and help, as if he was his good friend. Even Christ himself was tempted in this way; it was not that such emotions in him ever issued from doubt or mistrust in his Father's mercy, for in him was no root of faithlessness. Rather, during his anguish he had to submit to God's burning holiness and wrath. Remember how Matthew records him as twice praying, 'Let this cup pass from me' then 'nevertheless, not as I will but as you will' (26:39, 42); these two statements are plainly opposing. We find the same contrast in his cry, 'My God, my God' then, 'Why have you forsaken me?'

Therefore, I repeat: be comforted that it is no new thing when God's servants experience troubles and find themselves at times full of apprehension, yet at other times strong in faith. What Hezekiah experienced, King David also knew. Some of you may not really understand what I am saying, but nonetheless keep it in your memories; one day in the future it may stand you in good stead. For this is certain, though physical pain may be intense, there is as great a difference between bodily pain and pain of the soul, as there is between the Creator and the creature. Were you to feel just one touch of the consuming wrath of God in your soul, you would then rather choose every physical torment that has ever been devised. Yet on their own, these words alone I speak to you will have no effect; words can never soften the human heart unless the Lord himself by the power of his Spirit works in us. Therefore, I crave of God, and you must assist me by your prayers, that you may not be unfruitful hearers of the word. Realizing that there is a hell, may you so strive that you will never to be consigned to it.

The third lesson

Finally, notice that King Hezekiah teaches us a new way to pray; I beg you to take careful note of it. When his extremity is so intense that he cannot even frame words, for his speech is taken from him, he still continues to pray by lamenting and mourning, having recourse to the sounds made by a dove, a crane or a swallow; by differing sounds he expresses his anguish. You ask what kind of praying this is? I answer that sighing, grieving and lifting up of the eyes are as good a way to address God as any language spoken by our lips. The Lord understands the meaning of your sighs and groans better than you understand my words as I preach to you. You ask how this can be? I answer that it is his own Spirit that raises these sighs and groans, and causes the mourning of your soul. So I ask you, Does the Lord not know the meaning of his own

Spirit? The apostle Paul assures us of this in Romans.[33] Of course he knows the meaning of his own Spirit, so whether the Spirit moves us to sigh, to mourn, or to speak, the Lord understands all alike.

Therefore, use this method of prayer if the Lord visits you with some illness that is so serious you find yourself unable to find the words to pray; when you can neither lift up your hands to praise him, nor even raise your eyes to heaven, you can still let your groans come before him. It may be that you cannot even groan audibly, far less honour and glorify God with words. It may be that your heart has no strength to pray, neither are your lips able to utter praise; then let your hand or your arm or your eyes do it for you. For using one of the members of your body to combat the hardness of your heart is acceptable to God; and I do not doubt that he who raises a hand or arm to him, is enabled so to do by a special imparted grace, even though we may delay and struggle to make such a movement towards him.

If you can learn this, you will never be bereft of some means of praying. For prayer can sometimes be expressed through our tears, sometimes by sighs, sometimes by words and other times by gestures. But always ensure your spirit is well occupied, meditating upon God and spiritual things. Whether you are eating or drinking or resting or whatever, let your spirit always be mindful of God.

Knowing this, encourage yourself. I mean should the Lord visit you with such severity that your speech is taken from

---

[33] Rom. 8:26: 'Likewise the Spirit also helpeth our infirmities: for we knowe not what to praie as we oght: but the Spirit it self maketh request for vs with sighs, which can not be expressed' (GenB).

you, let the rest of your physical members honour him. And if you yourself are not afflicted by some physical ailment but you are visiting someone else who is, share this with them for their comfort, that God understands the language of gestures just as well as he understands the words we may use in prayer.

Hezekiah was not exempt from trouble or from trials or provocations of both body and soul. No one who resolves to live a godly life will avoid suffering. Those who set out on the path to heaven—be they some prince or just working folk—must enter by the strait gate and follow the narrow way. As for those who choose to follow the broad road, their state will continually deteriorate until, as the apostle says, they find that the Lord visits on them those very sins by which they have been provoking him. This is his just judgment: if you have angered him by adultery, he shall anger you by the same sin. Have you provoked him by shedding blood? By blood he shall provoke you. Have you angered him by blasphemy? He shall mete out to you the punishment due to blasphemy. The same with drunkenness. For every sin brings its own particular reprisal on the sinner. Therefore, if you would avoid the consequences of sin, resolve to avoid sin, so far as the Lord grants you grace to keep yourselves free from offending him. In this way he will give you joy and he may also grant you length of days here on earth; but, far better, he will give you everlasting joy in the hereafter, purchased for us through the righteous merits of Christ Jesus. To whom, with the Father and the Holy Spirit, be all praise and honour and glory for ever and ever. Amen.

The Fifth Sermon

Upon Isaiah Chapter 38

What shall I say? For he has spoken to me, and he himself has done it. I walk slowly all my years because of the bitterness of my soul. [16] O Lord, by these things men live, and in all these is the life of my spirit. Oh restore me to health and make me live!—Isaiah 38:15-16

IN our last lesson, well-beloved in Christ Jesus, the king returned in his song to the grief occasioned by his illness, taking up his lamentation and expressing his trouble in these words, 'My dwelling is plucked up and removed from me', meaning, 'My life is nearly ended, death is close, my departure is at hand.' He used two similes: the first was taken from a nomadic shepherd's tent. Just as the tent is dismantled, folded up and carried away, so his life was about to be folded up and taken away. So we are warned not to settle down here as if this life was a building with a permanent tenure;[1] we must always be ready to move, for we do not know at what

---

[1] See Sermon Four above and note 4.

hour the Lord will call us. All of us know that we must one day flit, for that is written into our consciences; therefore we cannot settle down in a frail dwelling that we cannot occupy for ever. Those who know that the Lord's summons must surely come will invest in the life beyond and prepare for it by sending on in advance their goods and their money. If it is wise to manage earthly investments carefully, how much more should we send ahead the wealth we may have, since the Lord will one day give us a permanent pasturage.[2] As it is true that the heart follows the wealth, let both heart and wealth be sent to heaven, where they may both meet us to our everlasting comfort. So be rich in God, be rich in good works, for that kind of wealth is able to accompany you and will stand you in good stead here on earth and afterwards in heaven.

Hezekiah's second simile was taken from the weaver and his loom. As the weaver may cut off his fragile material prematurely, so the king means by his words, 'I have been doing my work, weaving at the loom of my life, now the fragile material I have made is going to be cut off from the loom uncompleted; by my evil life I have brought upon myself this sudden and untimely end, thus I have hastened the grim reaper'. It is true that bodily diseases, and the chief diseases of the soul, flow from sin. Thus as death entered the world

---

[2] 'Pasturage': Bruce's phrase is 'the Lord giveth us lesour'; 'lesour' is a legal term used in the sixteenth and seventeenth century in the *tendendam* clauses of grants of grazing land. The intended imagery is that in heaven we are led into permanent tenure of 'green pastures and beside still waters' as in Psalm 23. See note 12 in Sermon Four above; Bruce himself had surrendered his right to several lucrative earthly 'lesours'.

by sin,[3] so by multiplication of sin death is hastened. Sin shortens our lives and makes our days evil; sin fills our years with grief and sorrow and brings in its wake a thousand cares; sin entraps us in a multiplicity of unprofitable labours and weakens our bodies with deceitful pleasures; sin vexes our minds with terrors beyond description. If this good youthful king had occasion to say that the evil of his life had spurred him on towards his death, what may our young nobility say? If it is true that one single sin, shedding blood, cuts off half a man's life (as the Psalmist says[4]), how much more shall a multitude of sins committed by one person shorten his days? Sacrilegious blasphemy, shedding the blood of a man whose lawful wife has been taken, together with innumerable other sins—shall not all this shorten the miserable life of the one who is guilty of them? What such a person fears most and would fain avoid at any cost, is the final judgment; yet he runs headlong towards it! As for the profane multitude, we see them indulging in two vices, gluttony and drunkenness; they two hasten on their death. The fact is that there is no one who is not subject to some sin or other that is shortening the thread of his life, and so leading him more rapidly towards the very end he wants to avoid.

Well, I will not enlarge further on the causes of premature departure of a man's life. Nevertheless, take heed of what I say, whether you walk in God's mercy or in the midst of your own sins; if the latter, it is the most dreadful judgment to be

[3] Rom. 5:12.

[4] Psa. 55:23: 'And thou, o God, shalt bring thē downe into the pit of corruptiō: the blooddie, & deceitful men shal not liue halfe their dayes: but I wil trust in thee' (GenB).

abandoned and entirely alone. But just now mercy is offered, and therefore any who would be transferred from death to life, use diligently the days that are still granted to you.

In the second part of our study I pointed out to you the ferocity of Hezekiah's sickness; I also explained that his fever raged so hotly as to make him think God was a devouring lion, ready to grind his very bones to powder; it made him expect that both his body and soul would be taken from him by evening of that very day. I tried to show you that these thoughts could not have arisen simply from physical pain, but from a far deeper pain than one that could ever come from some human illness. Of all the troubles that beset a man, the afflictions of the conscience are the greatest, not least when added to the guilt of sin is the merest glimpse of the unspeakable anger and indignation of the living God. It would appear by these silent voices in his soul that King Hezekiah felt the merest touch of this wrath whereby God seemed to be only a consuming fire.

At times God chooses to bring his dear children to these extremities so that, feeling something of the pangs of hell, they will realize how precious the death of Christ ought to be to them, how deeply they are indebted to him and what obligation is now laid upon them towards him who stood between them and so bitter a punishment. Such extremities teach us how easy it is for the Lord to subdue the pride of the flesh and to beat down the depravity of our corrupt natures. In a manner of speaking, in the space of twelve hours this glorious king was brought to the brink of the grave and to the doorway of desperation. The Lord does not need fire or sword to bring low the proudest of men, but simply uses what lies deep within our human natures; he is able to use that which we cherish to become our severest torments, for we all carry within our souls either some venomous serpent or else some other deadly virus[5] which will end up destroying us unless the Lord in his mercy intervenes on our behalf.

Last of all, we saw how the king acted in this greatest extremity. Even though God appeared to him to be a fire in his soul, he nevertheless cast himself upon this same God, to whom he did not need words to express the grief and trouble of his heart, for the benefit of his speech had been taken from him, but by sighing and groaning like a dove or swallow or crane. That was how he prayed with gestures and the lifting up of his face. When he was able to speak and pray, his few words were really unnecessary: 'I am oppressed; be my pledge of safety', or else usher me out of this life.

What he wanted to communicate to God was something like this: 'The intensity of my illness and the heat of my fever is so great that it is too overpowering for my body; therefore, because my own physical resources cannot save me, I am fleeing to you, my Creator. Because it was you who made me, it must be easy for you, Lord, to restore my life! So from you I crave healing and the prolongation of my days. You have begun a work through me, and so I plead that you will complete that work, for the glory of your name and the strengthening of your kirk.'

From this we learned first that during their greatest troubles God's servants burst into seemingly contradictory voices,

---

[5] I have used the word 'virus' though it was not known until 1599. Bruce's clause reads: '...we carry within us ane viper or other quhilk shall destroy the soul...'

uttering words sometimes of deep doubt but then of calm confidence. In verse 13 God appeared to have been like a raging lion, but then in the next verse he runs to this same God and casts himself upon him. Therefore doubting and confidence may both have a place in the self-same soul. Every servant of God has experience of this. Indeed, the Lord's children will always have known seasons of being beset with doubts, yet God in his mercy preserves and sustains them. You see, although nothing is pleasing to God except what is perfect, as long as we are here on earth and our faith is always imperfect, it cannot but be that the soul will be at times assailed with doubts. As faithful souls search the Scriptures and understand that perfection is our ultimate goal, yet know how far short they fall from that perfection, it is obviously all too possible for them to be vexed with doubts.

Quite apart from the sort of trial that Hezekiah had, when we believers become aware of the sin still imbedded in our fallen flesh, and the wrong desires that tempt us, and when we consider how God hates all sinfulness, how can we not have doubts? So we are caught in this dilemma: looking at ourselves, we doubt, but looking to the mercy of God in Christ Jesus, we believe. That illustrious vessel of the Lord expressed it like this in 2 Corinthians 4:8, 'We are afflicted in every way, but not crushed; perplexed, but not driven to despair.' Though the good apostle acknowledged doubting, yet he denied despair, for despair hacks at the pillars of our hope, and consequently at our faith; therefore despair cannot share a place in the soul with faith.

What I mean by 'doubting' is that emotion that is comprised of the errors, hesitations and wrestling whereby the soul is troubled—wrestling, that is, between hope and despair. Yet all these imperfections in us are freely pardoned through the righteous merits of Jesus Christ, without which we have no salvation. Those who understand what I am talking about, comfort yourselves with this; but those of you who have yet to experience it, learn and remember these truths so that you will not be taken unawares if it pleases the Lord to visit you as he did Hezekiah and the apostle.

A second lesson from this final part of last week's sermon was this: we learned from King Hezekiah that it is not always necessary to pray to God using words or speech, but we can equally well have recourse to God with lamentations, sighs, groans, and gestures such as lifting up our eyes to him. For the Lord understands our tears and sighs just as well as he understands our speech. How can this be? Because those sighs and tears are raised in our hearts by his own Spirit, and of course he knows what his own Spirit means. Therefore, when you cannot praise him with your lips, let any and every part of your body praise him. Remember, there is no other route into heaven other than through troubles. It does not matter what a man's estate is, whether he be emperor, king, prince or common man, all must enter into life through the strait and narrow gate. Only those appointed for damnation follow the broad way—but oh, how terrible is the anguish that awaits them at the end! They enjoy a brief time of pleasure but it is rewarded by eternal sorrow; therefore, their condition is to be lamented rather than envied. You who are heading for the city which has foundations and for that kingdom that cannot be shaken, do not be wearied as you go on along the strait path; whatever trials the Lord lays upon you accept with patience, for these are but pledges of mercy such as bring us to tread the same way Christ Jesus trod, in whom alone is true comfort and salvation. Thus far we went in last Sunday's sermon.

Our Bible passage for today

> What shall I say? For he has spoken to me, and he himself has done it. I walk slowly all my years because of the bitterness of my soul. [16] O Lord, by these things men live, and in all these is the life of my spirit. Oh restore me to health and make me live!

Here in the fifteenth verse, the king lingers and muses upon the greatness of God's blessing upon him. Overwhelmed in admiration for the wonderful works of God, he bursts forth in praise and thankfulness, 'What shall I say?' The briefest of exclamations, indicating that his heart was so full of emotion that he could not find words to express himself. 'What shall I say?'—as if he wanted to say, 'Where will I find words to relate all that has happened? Where shall I borrow praise that I may respond to such goodness and kindness brought to me by this God of mine? I no sooner had turned to him with tears flowing down my face than he accepted me, and promised me his kindly, merciful protection all the rest of my days. How is it possible for me to acknowledge such blessings in word, let alone in deeds? Indeed, I find it quite impossible for my tongue to utter what is in my heart. But even though I cannot as I would, I shall praise you, Lord, as I am able, and as much as you have given me the grace to do so.'

Three things that Hezekiah acknowledges in his thanksgiving

He had learned from his predecessor, David, a notable kind of thanksgiving when that king was in a similar situation, and also burst forth in praise: 'What shall I render to the LORD for all his benefits to me?'[6] Here is a form of praise in which this good king makes three acknowledgements.

First and very briefly, he confesses that the blessing he had received was free, gratuitously bestowed upon him, without any of his own doing. Yes, he acknowledged that he had received a completely undeserved bounty.[7]

Second, he admits that he had done nothing himself to deserve this blessing—neither a word nor a deed; thus he is scarcely able to render praise for it.

Third, he testifies that even though he is not able to burst into the praise of this great God in the manner in which he longed to do and in true proportion to the worthiness of the blessing, yet he should not do nothing. Surely, even in these few words he uses he displays the signs of a more thankful heart than if he had used a cart-load of phrases or uttered millions of sentences. It is not the verbosity of the tongue the Lord looks for, rather he has an eye to the inward condition of the heart and of the spirit, because he himself is a spirit.

---

[6] Psa. 116:12.

[7] Bruce's words that I have translated as 'undeserved bounty' are 'plat contrare'; 'plat', meaning 'design' or 'plan', was used to denote a scheme inaugurated in 1573 for reorganizing stipends in post-Reformation Scotland; stipends were derived from the teinds (tithes) paid by owners of estates and farms. A slightly different translation might have been 'an unexpected bonus'.

THE WAY TO TRUE PEACE AND REST

Therefore the Lord was pleased with this king's heart, even though his words were so few.

Since the animal sacrifices of the old law have now ceased, there is not a spiritual sacrifice more acceptable to God than that of praise and thanksgiving. For such sacrifices sanctify not only ourselves, but also every blessing that the Lord bestows upon us. For what obtains regarding our food and drink also holds true for all the benefits we receive, every one of which is a pledge of God's mercy in Christ Jesus. The apostle testifies to this in 1 Timothy 4:3-5 where he writes that 'foods that God created are to be received with thanksgiving', for they are 'made holy by the word of God and prayer'. As this is true of the food God's creation provides for us, so it is true of all the rest of his blessings.

Three things to be marked in thanksgiving

When I read the king's thanksgiving, 'What shall I say?' three things are at once evident. First, there is the wonderful goodness of God. We easily see the divine goodness in this form of praise. For God has the right to expect our life, soul and body, as well as every single thing we do, for his benefit. Yet he accepts a simple sort of praise and thanksgiving; as long as our hearts are right, even though our words are a babble that is acceptable to him.

Second, there is our lamentable ingratitude, for even though feeble and inadequate thanksgiving is acceptable to God, yet we rarely offer to him even that. It is intolerable ingratitude on our part that it never occurs to many of us even to think about thanking him, let alone actually doing it. So what are the consequences of our thanklessness? Though we may possess the Lord's gracious benefits, our consciences are not clear. More, it will ultimately come to pass that God's blessing will be withdrawn from our material prosperity, and the next generation of our godless family may even find God's curse upon their wealth. And the rot first set in on account of our base ingratitude.

I will not be gainsaid on this. I am quite certain that all who have received the blessing of God, and whose hearts are right with him, will engage in returning thanks and will live gratefully. A conscience that is clear never shakes off the memory of the Lord's goodness. Therefore it follows that those who never turn to God in thankfulness for his manifold benefits have self-evidently received his blessings in vain; their hearts and consciences are not right with him. That is why his good hand will be withdrawn and their wealth will be cursed, if not in their lifetime for the Lord is longsuffering, certainly in the next generation. Therefore, to acknowledge that his many blessings are truly appreciated, give praise and thanksgiving for them, and do not seek to accumulate more unless you can do so in good conscience.

Third, there is the arrogance of God's opponents in churches dominating some nations in Europe, largely untouched by the Reformation. This arrogance of which I speak concerns those who imagine that not only should they give God thanks, but that they are also able to satisfy him by their own good deeds in return for his. When by their various good works they estimate they have made him sufficient satisfaction to be justified, they then proceed to try and build up a surplus of merit. This they call 'supererogation'.[8] Such

---

[8] 'In Roman Catholic moral theology, acts which are not enjoined

works of so-called supererogation are a superlative folly and inexpressible madness, for while all the great servants of God have found that our works are never sufficient to merit God's grace, those who seek to accumulate a surplus of good works imagine they can thereby measure up to equal his infinite goodness. But let us move on.

The greatness of the benefit received

The next words read, 'He himself has spoken to me, and he himself has done it.' The king is saying, 'The Lord promised, and he has kept his promise. He both said it and did it so that the whole glory of the event might belong to him. I was told that I would die, but then the Lord came a second time and gratuitously brought his word again: freely he spoke and freely he kept that word, for even though all the world is false, he is true and faithful.' So you see how, in these two simple statements, the king brings out the mercy and truth of God—the mercy of God through his promise, and his truth in keeping and performing his promise.

You may ask, 'What do you mean by "mercy"?' I mean his mercy in promising freely, for he is debtor to no man, so that whatever he promises is gratuitous. For none of us have any claim to better conditions than were given to his chosen people. Those conditions are clearly set out in Deuteronomy

---

as of strict obligation, and therefore are not simply good as opposed to bad, but better as opposed to good ('*opera meliora*')... The term [supererogation] was probably not used until the Middle Ages... This doctrine was repudiated by the Reformers and in the Thirty-nine Articles (XIV), which asserts that "Works of Supererogation cannot be taught without arrogancy and impiety".' (*Oxford Dictionary of the Christian Church*, 3rd ed. OUP, 2005) p. 1570. See also Calvin, *Institutes*, III.14.12-21.

28 and the promises for obedience and curses for disobedience; also in Exodus 32 where we read of the idolatry of the
golden calf; and in Isaiah 48 which records the Lord's call to
Israel. In effect, God is saying there to his people, 'I knew how
stubborn you were, I could see that the sinews of your neck
were of brass and your face of iron; I knew you would be false
and unfaithful to me; notwithstanding, I freely promised to
be your God and down the generations I have kept my promise.' And again in Isaiah 53, he says, as it were, 'It is I, yes, it
is I who puts away your iniquities.' And in 43:25, he says, 'I,
I am he who blots out your transgressions for my own sake,
and I will not remember your sins.' If this be true for the
natural olive branches, how much more is it true for us who
have been grafted in? For we have no means of escaping the
judgments of God apart from his mercy freely offered to us
through the blood of Christ Jesus.

'It is God', says the king, 'who has done this.' It is as if he
said, 'All men are liars, God alone is true.' For he has said that
before one jot is taken from his promise, the entire world will
be turned upside down and the whole course of nature thrown
into turmoil.[9] See in verse 8 what happened to the sun! From
this we learn that there is not lacking in God either the power
or the will; it is we who lack an open hand to receive in faith
his promises. Thus even though there are wagon-loads of sure
and certain promises, it is not possible for these promises to
avail us anything unless the Spirit opens up a way for himself
and the Lord creates faith in our souls. Therefore your concern and diligence should be to crave that along with your
hearing of the word, the Lord would be pleased to add the

---

[9] Bruce is paraphrasing Matthew 24:35: 'Heauen and earth shal passe
away: but my wordes shal not passe away.' (GenB)

working of his Spirit, so that, faith being wrought and the heart fully opened, we may lean and repose steadfastly upon the faithful promises of God.

The effect that issues from the benefit

In the second part of verse 15, he tells of the blessed effect flowing from this blessing from God: 'I shall from henceforth all the rest of my years walk overpassing the bitterness of my soul.'[10] Hezekiah means: By this benefit, the grief of my conscience and the terrors and troubles of my soul are removed! He makes no mention of other aspects of the blessing such as the healing of his body and the promise of a stable kingdom, both of which were included. He only speaks of what moved him the most, namely, the grief of his conscience. This bitterness made such a deep impression on his soul that in verse 17 he calls it 'great bitterness'. For when God's judgments make a deep impression on the soul, they also make a deep mark that sin cannot easily erase. When the memory of that divine judgment is fresh, it is easy to be full of gratitude; it is easy to apply ourselves to the work God has given us; it is easy to stand in awe lest we fall again into the hands of God. On the other hand, if we blot out that memory of God's chastening, we sink again into the very mire out of which we were delivered. Therefore, I commend you to crave of God a sanctified memory so that you do not forget God's severity, which you have either seen in others or else experienced yourselves.

[10] This is Bruce's paraphrase of the translation in the Bible he used: 'I shal walke weakely all my yeres in the bitterness of my soule' (GenB); ESV translates: 'I walk slowly all my years because of the bitterness of my soul.'

Then such memories may enable you to be thankful to the Lord, and cause you to stand in awe of him, lest you fall into the hands of him who can also be a consuming fire.

A burst of praise

> O Lord, by these things men live, and in all these is the life of my spirit. Oh restore me to health and make me live!

Now comes teaching in verse 16 that is both necessary and notable for us today. I shall deal with it first generally and then more particularly.

First, the king praises the word on account of the good it works generally for all humanity. He says, 'O Lord, by these things men live.' He means that by the power of the word we are all enabled to enjoy the benefits of the natural life that we live in these mortal bodies here on earth. For the Lord's voice called on things that were not, that they might come into being. By his word he created heaven and earth; by his word he gave human beings life and breath; by his word he assigned to us the earth, the seasons and the bounds of our habitation. All this that mankind, created in the image of God, might seek the God who is not very far from us. For as the apostle says in Acts 17:28, 'In him we live and move and have our being.' And as this is true with respect to our actual existence, it is also true in our enjoyment of this life we have been given, for by the blessing of his word our lives are sustained. 'For our life consists not only in food and drink, but in every word that proceeds out of the Lord's mouth',[11] that is, from all that the Lord has appointed to nourish us. For even if all food and

---

[11] The allusion is to Matt. 4:4, cited from Deut. 8:3.

drink were removed, he would be able to create stones that could nourish us. This is the first reason why this good king acknowledges the blessed effects of the word and praises it.

Second, he moves forward from the general to the particular, and now praises the word from his own personal experience. He says that in the word's benefits is the sum total of the life of his soul: 'in all these is the life of my soul'. What he means is that through the Lord's words and works, his truth and mercy, his promises and faithfulness, the life of his soul is sustained. In effect, the king is saying, 'Not only do I have this human life which I live in this frail body, but by the benefit of the word I have a much more precious life, that life of my soul and spirit that distinguishes me from others, has conferred on me a unique status as king, and has even given me a foretaste of the heavenly life which is eternal.'

You see, as our natural bodies live and then die, there is also life and death for the soul. On the one hand, it is possible for a man to be physically alive but his soul to be dead; on the other hand, when a man's body dies, his soul may live on. 'Except the soul be born again of the Spirit of life, you shall never see the face of God.' Until the soul is quickened by the Spirit of life, it is dead, dead in sin and in the evil desires of the flesh, as the apostle says in Ephesians and Colossians.[12] In other words, the soul as well as the body can be dead; the soul can be as void of spiritual and heavenly life as is a dead body void of natural life. The apostle's words to which I have referred are, 'Dead in sin, dead in trespasses, dead in the uncircumcised lusts of the flesh.' When someone is dead, the life has been extinguished so that there is neither half of

[12] Eph. 2:1-6; Col. 2:12-13.

life, nor a quarter of life, nor even a breath of life. That is exactly how it is when a man's soul is dead, because, being dead, by definition there is not in him even the tiniest spark of heavenly life. And if there is not so much as a spark of life, where is that half or quarter life of which some Roman Catholics speak? They suggest that death is not actual death but impaired or limp. Yet the apostle says plainly that death is death and that therefore any spiritual life must be wholly extinguished. Consequently any ability of the will towards goodness and all sight of God in Christ Jesus are completely extinct. So the state of a soul that is dead continues until that moment when the Spirit of life does his work; he is the same Spirit of life who is within the body of Christ, who alone can free us from the body of sin and the body of death that pertains to our fallen natures, as the apostle says in Romans.[13]

How can I know if the Holy Spirit is in my life?

Do you want to know if your soul is alive to God, and how this may be perceived? There are many effects given in the Scriptures such as the fruit of the Spirit recorded in Galatians 5. But I shall offer you three others by which you may discern the presence of life in your soul. The first we shall consider is an inward peace of conscience.

When you find your conscience refreshed and your soul renewed after the painful experience of deep conviction of sin, then you may be assured that your soul has been quickened, for this is the effect of the Holy Spirit's work. And this is also the peace that passes understanding of which the world is

---

[13] Rom. 8:2, 'For the law of the Spirit of life has set you free in Christ Jesus from the law of sin and death.'

ignorant. The more this peace increases in your soul, the more the new life fills it. Likewise the more you resist the desire for sin and seek to cast it out along with all the baggage that clings to it, the more your conscience is at rest. In a word, the thing that troubles the soul and disturbs the conscience is the sin on which we must turn our backs, for that is what comes between us and God in whom alone is true rest, peace and quietness. Therefore our chief endeavour should be to expel the enemy, the monster sin, and to possess the saving elixir of peace that passes all understanding.

The second effect to bring us assurance that our souls have been made alive to God is the joy and rejoicing when we are harassed by troubles or trials. We know from our own experience that joy during trials is not a normal reaction, for humanly speaking troubles produce sorrow, sadness and depression. Conversely, when our spirits are able to rejoice in spite of trouble, this is clear evidence of the blessed Spirit within who alone quickens the soul. The joy that the Spirit can bring can cause us not only to rejoice in our trials, but also to glory as did the apostle.[14] For surely through the cross of Christ comes our only joy, and the shame we bear for his sake is our only honour. It is in this that we perceive the great honour to which the Lord has called us, that he not only gives us faith to believe his word, but he permits us also to suffer for him. A word of caution: I have not here been speaking about any kind of trouble we may experience, but only those troubles—I mean trials—that we endure in Christ's cause

---

[14] The allusion is probably to Eph. 3:13 which in Bruce's Bible reads, 'Wherefore I desire that ye faint not at my tribulations for your sakes, which is your glorie' (GenB). See also 1 Pet. 1:8.

and for righteousness' sake, trials that are undeserved and not brought on us by ourselves. For the troubles which are our own fault will certainly not bring us joy!

The third evidence that brings the assurance of a quickened soul is love for God and hatred of evil. Where else but in our souls is this love kindled when we begin to know and love God and to taste of him. For it is not really possible to love him until we have tasted his sweetness. This love begins the work of making us into the likeness of God, for God is love, and, as John says, 'If love dwells in your heart, God also dwells in your heart, for God is love.'[15] Therefore this love is a sure pledge of a quickened soul. Of necessity, the converse holds true: when we love God, we will also hate evil.

We should all consider examining ourselves to ascertain whether the Holy Spirit has worked in our hearts to produce, in some measure at least, any of these three evidences of his presence in us. Even though the effect of his presence in our lives is very small, it is sure confirmation that he has begun his work in us, and the work that has been begun will be perfected by God. For example, even if our love for God and hatred of evil are very small, we may still be sure that Christ is dwelling in our hearts by faith and our souls have been quickened by his Spirit. Those of you who are aware of this—how I long that all of you were aware of it—must strive to nourish and strengthen this new life. Do not be weary in so doing, but press on in this life in the Spirit. Do not sow to the flesh and do not persist in its lusts and desires; the apostle warns us in Romans 6:16-19 of the consequences of remaining as slaves to sin, namely, impurity, lawlessness, confusion and finally

[15] 1 John 4:16.

death of both body and soul. As the same apostle urges, sow rather to the things of the Spirit so that you may reap the life everlasting.[16]

How the Spirit is nourished in us and how also he can be quenched

The Holy Spirit is strengthened and nourished in our lives when we nourish the light and knowledge of God in Christ Jesus, edify ourselves in our most holy faith and continue faithfully in daily prayer. Conversely, we banish the Spirit in our lives when by wrong-doing we banish the knowledge of God and so extinguish the light of Christ, thus weakening our faith and persisting in neglecting prayer. When those means of nourishing and strengthening the Spirit's presence are cast aside, then our awareness of his presence is lost. Therefore, all who would walk with the Lord must be eager to increase their knowledge of God, to strive to do what is right, to be attentive to God's word thereby building themselves up in the faith, and constantly to pray for grace and mercy.

Returning to Hezekiah's words, 'the life of my spirit and restore me and make me live', I take it that he is referring to this same life of the soul of which we have been thinking. He had experience of this life that God has promised as we read in Romans 1:16, 'the power of God for salvation to everyone who believes'. Moses speaks of this same life when he says, 'Set your hearts upon this word, for it is not a vain word; it is your life and felicity.'[17] Our Master says, 'The words that I

---

[16] Gal. 6:7-8.

[17] Deut. 32:46-47: 'Set your hearts vnto all the wordes which I testifie against you this day … For it is no vaine worde concerning you, but it is your life, and by this worde ye shal prolong your dayes in the land' (GenB).

speak are spirit and life', therefore John records him as being 'the word of life' and 'the bread of life'.[18] In the same place Peter says, 'Lord, to whom shall we go? You have the words of eternal life.'[19] Christ says that 'as the Father has life in himself, so he has granted the Son to have life in himself.'[20] From this the apostle can say, '"The first man Adam became a living being"; the last Adam became a life-giving spirit.'[21] Because we are made recipients of his Spirit through the ministry of his word, it is called the word of the Spirit. That is why the apostle implies in 2 Corinthians 3 and 4 that he was counted as a minister of the Spirit.[22] If any desire further praise of the word, that is the subject of Psalm 19 where the attributes and effects of the word are set down.

When we consider the precious influence of the word, and on the other hand we observe so much unhappiness in many lives, I am sure that it must astonish any Christian heart to realize how the Lord can regard our contempt with such long-suffering patience. For in the past in our land, when there was scarcely any chance to feed on this bread of life, men yearned for it and with diligence and zeal compassed both land and sea, disregarding distance and cost, to hear it; then, as it were, they forced themselves upon us to gain a hearing and to bring to us this word of life, turning our land upside down.

But now, alas, when it has pleased the Lord to offer us an abundance of this spiritual food, we so despised the bounty and generosity of our good God, that we turn his grace and

---

[18] John 6:35, 48, 63; 5:24.
[19] John 6:68.
[20] John 5:26.
[21] 1 Cor. 15:45.
[22] The allusion is to 2 Cor. 3:17-18 and 4:1, 13.

mercy into judgment and punishment upon our heads. As for the vast majority of our nation, they disdain it so maliciously that they would prefer to return to the leaven of the Pharisees and align themselves with those whose only offerings of spiritual sustenance are chants, vestments, masquerading and intonations in a language they don't understand. They think they can feed their souls by such mockery of God!

Our nation's aristocracy

As to the gentlemen, the earls, lords and barons, they are so intoxicated with sacrilege that, rather than part with all their former superstition, they will throw away the life of their souls. Indeed, though our parliament now prescribes that the preaching of the word must be maintained at their expense, they refuse to make their lawful contributions,[23] preferring rather to lose their souls a hundred times over before parting with a single halfpenny for the kirk. This is how it is for a large part of our nation, so it is only because the Lord himself wonderfully maintains the gospel light among us that the ministry continues to be exercised in Scotland. There is little or no nutritious food in the pulpits, only raw husks served up by most preachers.

Is not the judgment of God spoken of in 2 Thessalonians 2:9-12 descending upon us? 'The lawless one is by the activity

---

[23] The reference is to teinds (tithes): 'In Scotland teinds were the tenths of certain produce of the land appropriated to the maintenance of the church and clergy. At the Reformation most of the church property was acquired by the Crown, nobles and landowners. In 1567 the Privy Council of Scotland provided that a third of the revenues of lands should be applied to paying the clergy of the reformed Church of Scotland.' (http://en.wikipedia.org/wiki/Tithe)

of Satan ... with wicked deception for those who are perishing, because they refuse to love the truth and so be saved.' It is God who sends this 'strong delusion so that they believe what is false' and have 'pleasure in unrighteousness'. O unhappy and accursed land that has so abused the merciful calling and boundless generosity of God!

It is a cause for astonishment to see what is happening and to consider our great ingratitude. The more education increases among us the more men's consciences decay, as if conscience and knowledge could not co-exist in the same breast. Look at what is happening: the increase in the light in men's minds has apparently banished their consciences; yet before that light came consciences could be stirred. How can it be that as light increases its effect decreases. That this should be is beyond our understanding. Will not the outcome be quite terrible? Is it not amazing that the more our land is watered by that saving, heavenly dew, the harder men's hearts become! Many are heading towards a final conflagration; for the greater our contempt of the things of God, the greater will be the destruction. When well-watered ground produces only thorns and briers, the gardener's only recourse is to burn up such rank growth with a fire. Since our deeds testify that we are nothing but thorns, we cannot escape the flames unless the Lord intervenes to work among us in some unexpected manner. The longer judgment is delayed, the hotter will be the blaze once the fire is kindled, since our contempt is so great.

Therefore the Lord give you all grace that, knowing there is a hell and eternal anguish, you may so strive to escape it that you will change completely the direction of your living.

But that can only happen if the Lord works in our lives by his Spirit, puts our sins behind his back and assures us of his forgiveness through the blood of Christ. So I must plead with you, and you with me, that salvation may be a reality for us all, and in the compassion of his mercy we may avoid that terrible damnation—O! may the Lord preserve us from it for Christ Jesus his Son's sake! To whom, with the Father and the Holy Spirit, be all honour and praise, now and for ever. Amen.

The Sixth Sermon

Upon Isaiah Chapter 38

*O Lord, by these things men live, and in all these is the life
of my spirit. Oh restore me to health and make me live!* ¹⁷
*Behold, it was for my welfare that I had great bitterness; but
in love you have delivered my life from the pit of destruction, for you have cast all my sins behind your back.* ¹⁸ *For
Sheol does not thank you; death does not praise you; those
who go down to the pit do not hope for your faithfulness.*
¹⁹ *The living, the living, he thanks you, as I do this day; the
father makes known to the children your faithfulness.* ²⁰ *The
LORD will save me, and we will play my music on stringed
instruments all the days of our lives, at the house of the LORD.*

²¹ *Now Isaiah had said, 'Let them take a cake
of figs and apply it to the boil, that he may recover.'*
²² *Hezekiah also had said, 'What is the sign that I shall go up to
the house of the LORD?'*—Isaiah 38:16-22

IN our last lesson, well-beloved in Christ Jesus, the king was
in the second part of his song and we saw how he began by
bursting forth in praise of God. He then spoke of two great

benefits he had received from the Lord: the comfort he had found, and the word of God as the source of that comfort. So great was his admiration for the wonders of God's works that he exclaimed, 'What shall I say?' Such a brief comment, for he was lost for words to express how he felt! Yet though that sentence is so short, nevertheless he could not have described his gratitude any better even if he had used a million words. For true gratitude is not measured by syllables or sound, but by the attitude of the soul and mind. When the Lord sees that the heart is truly thankful, just a few words of gratitude are acceptable to him.

Nevertheless, in the king's brevity he did mention three things. First, the blessing was free and gratuitously bestowed; second, he had done nothing to deserve it either in word or deed; third, although he could never repay God for his goodness, there was something he could and would do, and that was to praise God in as far as his Spirit enabled him, for it is not possible that a good conscience and a godly soul can ever forget the Lord. The moment always comes when the faithful thank God for all his benefits. Indeed, those who forget or just never express gratitude to the Lord betray the fact that they have never genuinely laid hold of the riches of God's grace; the only wealth they possess is of this world and will one day be cursed, either in their own lifetime or that of those who inherit their money then waste it. If you would avoid such a curse, learn to thank God for all his benefits that you may enjoy them with his blessing on you and your families.

Next, you will remember, Hezekiah continued on the theme of the great blessing he had received. Again, he had two points: first, 'He said it', and second, 'He himself has done it.'

He said it in his promise and he did it when he fulfilled his promise. It was all of him so that the whole glory of the word should belong to him. The Lord said it freely, for the king himself confessed that he did not deserve it; and he did it just as freely by keeping his promise. If the whole world was false, God would nevertheless remain true. So Hezekiah speaks of the mercy and the truth of God: his mercy in promising and his truth in accomplishing. All of the Lord's promises flow from his mercy, and all his accomplishments flow from his truth. Why from his mercy? Because he is debtor to no man. And why from his truth? Because he himself is truth, and there is no promise he ever makes that he does not keep. He would rather alter the course of nature (as in the sun's shadow turning back ten steps[1]) rather than his word fall short; and heaven and earth will pass away ere one jot or tittle of his promise fail.[2] Yet, notwithstanding this constancy and fidelity in God, none of his promises will avail us anything except the Lord prepare and sanctify our hearts through the gift of faith, so that we may perceive his truth. Even then all his manifold promises will benefit us nothing unless and until the Lord enables us to take and apply his gracious truth. Therefore all Christian people must resolve to plead with the Lord to prepare their hearts by faith so that, seeing him in our minds, and feeling him in our hearts, we may find there his truth and mercy, and repose in them for ever.

We continued last Sunday by considering the word of God. We saw that by it we have the benefit of this earthly life. Yet the king praised the word not only for his temporal life but

[1] Isa. 38:8.
[2] Matt. 5:18.

also because by it he had spiritual life. The two are conjoined, for there can be physical life yet at the same time the soul can be dead; in addition, though the body may be dead the soul may be alive, for when we leave the body behind our souls may rise to a better place. While the body's life stands in the presence of the soul, the soul's life stands in the presence of the Spirit of life. Unless our souls are born anew by the power of that Spirit of life, we can never behold the face of God or taste his joy. For by nature we are not merely mutilated and lame, we are altogether dead in sin. Just as a dead carcass has no life whatsoever, so the natural man has neither heavenly nor spiritual life. It stands to reason: when death has taken place, all life is completely extinguished. If the Spirit of life is no longer present, not even the faintest whiff of any holy thoughts or actions can come from that cadaver. Therefore, if there is not present even a breath of spiritual life, how can there be free-will to choose the right as Roman Catholics aver? So how can any holiness remain in a defiled nature? Therefore I say that we are dead until by our participation in the Spirit of life, which dwells in the body of Christ, we are set free from sin and death. Until that happens, none of us will ever ascend to the heavens and the presence of God. So, as I exhorted you last Sunday, I exhort you again today that you all search your hearts to see whether there is yet spiritual life within you, and I gave you three consequences of the Spirit's presence, so that you may have that assurance. I shall remind you of them.

The first was that you will find yourself renewed in your spirit and delivered from the guilt in your conscience and from the fear of sin; this work of the Spirit is called 'the peace that passes all understanding', of which the world knows nothing. Those who find in their hearts any trace of this, however small, need have no doubt—this new life has begun its work within them; the more this new life is augmented, the more shall the peace increase. This new life is augmented as we mortify sin, so make that your daily exercise. The more free we are from sin, the greater shall be the repose that our consciences will enjoy.

The second consequence of the Spirit's life within us is joy and rejoicing in our trials. Our old natures cannot console us when we are troubled; all they can do is to inflict upon us sorrow, unhappiness and grief. But when we find ourselves enduring trials and our spirits are nonetheless able to rejoice, this is evidence of the Spirit of life. I am not referring to those troubles we bring on ourselves, but only to the trials that we undergo for righteousness' sake and for the sake of Christ.

The third consequence of the Spirit's presence with us is that, on the one hand, we find we have a new love for God and for his faithful children; on the other hand, we also find we have developed a hatred for evil. When we are aware of these dispositions within ourselves, we need have no doubt but that the Spirit of life has quickened our souls. The contrary is also true: those who love wickedness and the company of vile men that allows them to mock the name of Christ, in them the devil still has full dominion.

We further learned that the Spirit of life was nurtured by increasing our knowledge of God, by edifying ourselves in our most holy faith and by our cultivating the practice of prayer. We must also encourage our spiritual lives by doing good, for in this way our faith is confirmed. Delight, therefore, in well-doing, for thereby you sow in the Spirit and not in the flesh.

Do not consort with those who are dishonest, far less with those who threaten the lives of others; those who share in the sins of evil men shall also share in their punishment and will reap shame and eternal condemnation. Whereas those who sow in the Spirit shall reap everlasting happiness.

I do not apologize for reminding you of these things, for they are of the utmost importance, and I earnestly long that you should consider them carefully. Reflect on the great benefits God has bestowed on our nation; reflect too on our gratitude but also on the lack of gratitude exhibited by much depraved conduct. Any Christian who places these on the weighing scales—God's favour and our base ingratitude—will most certainly be amazed at how the Lord permits such iniquity in our land to go so long unpunished. I reminded you how in times past when there were available just a few crumbs of the bread of life, our great men hastened to seek it, compassing both sea and land, sparing neither travel nor cost, in order to be grafted into the kingdom of Christ. But now there is an abundance of the bread of life, many deeply loathe it thereby abusing the liberality of God offered to us, and turning his grace and mercy into vengeance upon all our heads.

As for the working folk, we all know that they have already chosen to return to the leaven of the Pharisees, with its masquerades and playacting in a language they cannot understand. The nobles and gentry are no better: they are so drunken with sacrilege that rather than give up the genuflecting and incense, they hazard both their bodies and souls. None either see it or lament it. For myself, I am overwhelmed with amazement to see what is happening: the more the light in our land grows, the more men's consciences decay; it is as if knowledge of the truth and good consciences cannot co-exist. And of course this leads to a decline in their willingness to do good, which, in itself, bears testimony to the darkness in which those in the churches lived prior to the reformation of religion in our land. Part of my amazement is that when the gospel's light has shone upon us, the abandonment of conscience shall rise up to condemn us. So what will be the consequence of this return to Catholicism? The apostle tells us in Hebrews 6 that the ground that has been watered and refreshed with rain, but only produces briars and thorns whose only use is as fuel for the fire, shall be consumed in the day of the Lord's judgment.[3]

To apply this (though the judgment be delayed) there inevitably remains a complete burning up, and the fires of destruction will be hotter in proportion to such brightness of the gospel's light as there has been; for the brighter the light the greater the contempt, and the greater the contempt the heavier must the judgment be. And as I search my own heart, I constantly expect that unless the situation changes more significantly than it has done until now, our nation shall become a spectacle to other nations near and far. This is how far we proceeded in last Sunday's sermon. Today we take up Hezekiah's song from verse 16.

> O Lord, by these things men live, and in all these is the life of my spirit. Oh restore me to health and make me live! [17] Behold, it was for my welfare that I had great bitterness; but in love you have delivered my life from the pit

[3] Heb. 6:7-8: 'For the earth which drinketh in the raine that cometh ofte vpon it … But that which beareth thornes & briars, is reproued, and is nere vnto cursing, whose end is to be burned' (GenB).

of destruction, for you have cast all my sins behind your back. [18] For Sheol does not thank you; death does not praise you; those who go down to the pit do not hope for your faithfulness. [19] The living, the living, he thanks you, as I do this day; the father makes known to the children your faithfulness. [20] The Lord will save me, and we will play my music on stringed instruments all the days of our lives, at the house of the Lord. [21] Now Isaiah had said, 'Let them take a cake of figs and apply it to the boil, that he may recover.' [22] Hezekiah also had said, 'What is the sign that I shall go up to the house of the Lord?'

The great benefits of the word

In verse 16, the king continues to praise that same blessed word of God for the ways in which it had proved true in its promises to him. He says, in effect, 'By the benefit of the word I have obtained healing of my body, for as sickness had taken all my powers from me and robbed me of my strength, by the word's benefit I have been restored to my health, and my vigour has returned. That same word has not only restored me from my illness but continues to preserve me.'

So tracing the king's thoughts back to verse 15 where he says, 'For he has spoken to me', and then on into verse 16, first he ascribes the life of his body to the word, second he ascribes the life of his soul to the word, third both the health of body and soul are attributed to the word, and finally he ascribes to the word the continuance of the health of both his body and soul. Where else can comfort be found but in the word? Whatever any Christian heart may long for is to be found in the word. I say more: no human lips or heart can ever express the comfort that the soul derives from the word. No mouths are capable of describing the joy that is brought to the hearts of those in whom the Spirit is effectual.

Nevertheless, in spite of the inexpressible benefits that flow from the word of God, how many of you are running to this word to seek strength and consolation? Consider the godless multitude, indeed consider also those of us who profess faith. Do we not first try to find the help we need from elsewhere before we at length run to this word? It is only when human and natural means have failed us that we then have no other option than to run to the word. There are times when we are too late in running to the word and we are met with a refusal, and the door is slammed in our faces[4] as it was for the five foolish virgins. Well, this word is constantly sounded forth, therefore seek to grasp the needed strength and help from it in time; do not delay! Look to it that you listen to this word with the utmost reverence, and study to practise it daily more and more in your lives and conversations.

The Lord's chastening

[Verse 17 in the Geneva Bible begins, 'Beholde, for felicitie I had bitter grief', which could be understood as being slightly different to the ESV, 'Behold, it was for my welfare that I had great bitterness.' We should bear this in mind as we read Bruce's interpretation of the first part of the verse.]

In the seventeenth verse of this chapter, the king notes the occasion when he was stricken with the illness: it was during a time of peace after his deliverance from the hand of Sennacherib, and when he was at ease and enjoying wealth

---

[4] Bruce's phrase here is very vivid: 'the gates are steiked on our chafts'; 'chafts' is literally 'jaws' or 'jowls'!

in abundance. It was a time, he himself confesses, when he was blind to God's goodness and so abused the benefits of his deliverance. Then it was that God started to tweak his ear and cast him from the trauma of a fearful war and into the clutches of a terrible pestilence.[5] We should learn from the occasion of the king's sickness how hard it is for our human natures to cope with great wealth accompanied by good health. Indeed, it is quite impossible to drink such a cup for many years—unless the Lord by some means holds us in check—and not become like some overfed horse unable to work or carry its rider.

Therefore, seeing this is a malaise common to fallen humanity, we have to learn from the prayer of Agur, son of Jakeh. He craved two things of God: first, that God would remove from him 'falsehood and lying', that is, that he would remove from him and no longer remember his sins and preserve him from future evil; second, 'give me neither poverty nor riches', that is, that he would neither tempt him with over-abundance lest he should forget him, nor yet with great poverty lest he should revile him.[6] In other words, he asked of the Lord only his daily bread, that is, to give to each of us according to the needs of our vocation or profession just sufficient of temporary goods as is needful for our salvation and his glory. Then, in order that we may eschew the dangers of abundance that turn us away from God and be delivered from abject poverty that can cause us to blaspheme him, make your daily bread, just sufficient for your needs, your only crave of the Lord.

[5] See note 1 in Chapter 1 and the paragraph to which it refers.
[6] Prov. 30:8-9.

Ponder this, then, that a wealthy and successful king during a time of great prosperity should fall into neglect of God. It would not be surprising if this king who neglected the Lord was a ruler who was accustomed to assume absolute power over his subjects, who surrounded himself mainly with flatterers and who imbibed vanity as if it was water. But then consider many of our lords, who are not even kings, but who are so consumed by arrogant contempt for God that they constantly appear to be ready to join in a war against him. They will end up being as great enemies of the church as was Julian.[7] Well, in the case of the king we are considering, in the mercy of God he was chastised so that he should not fall into the condemnation of the reprobate. Had God not taken him to task and disciplined him, he would have experienced how fearful a thing it is to fall into the hands of him who is a consuming fire. The lords' tables may be spread with as much meat as they can eat, but they do not sit at the Lord's Table; the hour will come when they will curse the day of their birth and wish that they had never seen the light of day—unless, that is, the Lord intervenes in his mercy to bring to himself someone who had once blasphemed him.

The manner in which the king was delivered

At the end of verse 17 the king tells us how it was that the Lord 'delivered my life from the pit of destruction', how he had turned his grievous bitterness into a far better spirit of

---

[7] Flavius Claudius Julianus Augustus (AD 331–363). He was the last non-Christian Emperor of the Roman Empire; his rejection of Christianity in favour of Neoplatonic paganism caused him to be called Julian the Apostate by the church.

contentment. The way the Lord did it was this: 'you have cast all my sins behind your back'. He forgave his iniquity, for unless the Lord had forgiven his sins it would have been impossible for the bitterness in his soul and conscience to be removed. Thus, as soon as he turned to his God, acknowledging his past and in every kind of way seeking mercy—sometimes by words, sometimes by groans or tears or sighs, at times by dolorous lamentations, even by certain humble gestures—he obtained mercy as the Lord cast all his sins behind his back. What was it that moved the Lord to show him mercy? He tells us in the middle of verse 17. It was no merit in the king himself, for he deserved only condemnation. The Lord acted graciously out of love—'in love you have delivered my life'; in other words it was the kindness of God in Christ Jesus, the Messiah, that had been bestowed upon this king. There are three things we need to notice about the king's deliverance.

Sin is punished in the wicked and purged in the godly

First, we learn from the king that it is always sin that causes our misery, whether it be in our conscience, body or soul. This is undeniable, for the only thing God hates in us is our sin. Sin is the only thing that God punishes in the wicked; in the faithful, sin is the only thing that God corrects. It is only sin that is consumed by his burning jealousy; in believers, sin is the only thing he must purge. Take away all sin and all punishment shall cease. Let there be no more sin and the holy rites for cleansing shall no longer be necessary. Because Hezekiah acknowledged this and ran to God confessing his sin, he found mercy.

Therefore, learn the lesson: whatever affliction the Lord chooses to visit upon us, whether some bodily ailment or a troubled conscience, we must hasten along that highway to God, examine our past life, acknowledge our offences and run to the throne of grace for mercy. For whoever runs to that throne shall find mercy in the hour of his greatest need.

The second thing the king acknowledged was the remission of his sins, and this is the best and surest cure that can be applied to any affliction, for there can be no better or surer cure than to remove the cause of the trouble. When sin is the cause, removing sin removes the affliction. So many unhappy people in this world only look for some cure for their bodies when God afflicts them, as though only their bodies were to blame. They fail to examine their souls, when the fact is that the body can be a route to the soul. For if all is well with our souls, then the Lord will not afflict our bodies. Therefore, since the reason for God's chastisement is lurking in your soul, examine your soul and acknowledge the fault that is concealed there, and crave the Lord's mercy. Would to God we all learned this lesson! For if we all took it to heart, how much less would the divine afflictions rage amongst us.

The third thing that the king acknowledged was that his deliverance was not brought about by his own integrity. It was neither his own innocence nor good deeds, as he himself thought when he first prayed.[8] For in his prayer he seems to be making a show of his good deeds and integrity of life, but

---

[8] 'Then Hezekiah turned his face to the wall, and praied to the Lord, And said, I beseche thee, Lord, remember now how I haue walked before thee in trueth, & with a perfite heart, and haue done that which is good in thy sight: & Hezekiah wept sore' (Isa. 38:2-3, GenB).

here in verse 17 he resolves this apparent contradiction. So he lets us see that it was only by the mercy of God that he was delivered. Thus far the meaning of these words.

The form of speech

We are given a metaphor: 'You have cast all my sins behind your back.' Everything that is filthy and horrible we throw away out of sight so that we cannot see it. Because sin is the one thing that is an abomination to God, when he forgives us he casts our sins behind his back. Sin is the only thing from which he hides his face and it is sin alone that separates us from him. And what do we lose when his face is turned away from us? We lose true pleasure and perfect happiness, for only when we are at one with God can we experience real enjoyment. Thus we who are Christians should take diligent care to ensure that sin does not debar us from the open countenance of our God; that means ever craving mercy through the merits of Christ, so that by being favoured with the Lord's smile we may have that fullness of joy that lasts for ever.

But there is a second point to note in this metaphor. It is that 'he has cast *all* his sins behind his back' and not just some of his sins. No distinction is made between venial sins and mortal sins as if he forgives the former but not the latter. Absolutely all, without exception, that separates us from him has been put away. I think we can view our sins under three categories. The first kind are innate in us on account of our original corruption, that stinking pool and rotten root from which flow all its vile consequences. It was this corruption into which we were both conceived and born, causing us to be children of wrath and dead in sin. By the second category

I mean all emotions, thoughts and actions of our entire lives, whereby we deviate from the straight path and go far astray from our duty to God and our neighbour. In a word, under this second heading, I mean our actual sins.

The first category of original sin has profoundly affected us. Though we have the same kind of bodies as our first parents, our natures have been so scarred and deeply changed by our inner corruption that they no longer bear even a close resemblance to their state of perfection before the fall. That is why our human bodies are now subject to death—earth to earth and ashes to ashes. As to our souls, their original light of understanding has been turned to darkness, the integrity of our wills has been lost in wickedness, and the soul's righteousness that was once inclined only to good is now bent towards the resolve to do evil. In a word the perfect image of God in which we were first created and which once shone so brightly in man's soul has now been marred and all but lost.

Under the third category of sin I understand our failure to measure up to the standards given to us in the law. For before the fall we were able not only to abstain from sin, but also to accomplish all righteousness and so to conform perfectly to God's will in everything.[9] On account of our corruption we fail here also, and being guilty of all sorts of violations of the law, of necessity we are subject to death and condemnation. As the apostle says in Romans 5:12, the consequence of sin is death.

Hezekiah does not say that God has delivered him from the first two categories of sin, but not from the third. No, he

---

[9] I take it that here Bruce is alluding to Eph. 4:24: 'And put on the new man, which after God is created in righteousnes, and true holines' (GenB).

states that he has cast all his sins away and delivered him from death and condemnation. So mark well that this is the nature of God in Christ: from the moment when he begins to call his children to repentance and to work in their hearts, he does not forgive only certain of their sins, but he forgives all their sins, past, present and those to come; his grace comprehends the whole of their lives. In the parable of the Unmerciful Servant, the king forgave the man's entire debt (Matthew 18:23, 27). Through the atonement Christ has made he took upon himself the whole of our debt, not just a part of it; he became our 'cautiouner'[10] when he died for all of our sins. The satisfaction he made for sin was for the entire stock of guilt we have built up. Because the slate has been wiped clean, the Father asks for no more. In short, when he forgives us, he forgives all *simul et semel*.[11]

Only the Lord can open our hearts to his grace

By the proclamation of the gospel, forgiveness is freely offered to all; it is freely applied by the Holy Spirit, but is only grasped within the heart by the empty hand of faith. Only the Lord can cleanse our consciences, purify our hearts and open them as he did Lydia's; forgiveness of sins may be repeatedly offered to us, but we are only able to appropriate it as our consciences and souls are renewed in that sweetness and peace that flow from Christ. It doesn't matter how often the Lord's pardon is freely offered, men's consciences will be reluctant genuinely to accept it. We should all keep careful watch over ourselves lest

---

[10] Bruce's word, for which I can't find a contemporary English equivalent, means someone who stands in for a debtor and agrees to provide full security for the debtor and so to clear the debt on his behalf.

[11] The Latin phrase means 'at once and for all time'.

we confuse presumption with faith; the former can end up reducing a man to desperation.

Let us not be deceived by passive assent and superficial belief which are present in our fantasies. Justifying faith must open our hearts and be digested, so that the inner man may be genuinely renewed. For when someone only nibbles at the heavenly gift, however fervently the truth is proclaimed, the effect is passing and the taste is spat out. But when a person digests in his heart the grace of the heavenly gift in such a way that the stubbornness of his will is melted, his understanding renewed and his affections transformed, then he has no doubt about his acceptance before God; then, seeing him by faith and feeling his presence within, there is no tumult that can cause that person to run from the Lord; indeed, the greater the storms that beat against him, the nearer he will be drawn to Christ, for he now knows that there is a far better life with him beyond the grave.

To understand and appropriate all this is the duty of every believer. So all of you should try your hearts and minds, and petition God constantly by persistent suiting,[12] and so receive from him the grace that will open your heart to him. For none of us will ever be inclined to good unless our hearts are opened to feel his sweetness, and our wills and affections are transformed. Therefore crave that God will increase your faith that you may be able to withstand life's storms and remain steadfast.

---

[12] The language of the clause is from the law courts, so I did not want to drop the obsolete legal word 'suiting'; it means 'soliciting'.

A final point regarding this casting way of our sin

We must now enquire who it is who casts our sin behind his back? It is God the Father, the Son and the Holy Spirit who has done this; one God but three persons in one. No one else on earth can do this, only God. We read in the Gospels that the Pharisees knew that no one but God could forgive sins (Luke 5:21). On that occasion they charged Christ with blasphemy, accusing him of usurping the prerogative of forgiveness that belonged to God alone. But notice how the Lord reproved them: partly by not entering into discussion with them, and partly by performing a miracle of healing to ratify that what they had said was correct—only the God who had the right to forgive sins also had the power to heal. Even by natural reasoning we must agree that it is true that the God of heaven alone can forgive sins, just as only the creditor can cancel out a debt. By the same token, God alone has power to forgive, for sin is the transgression of his law, because our sins offend him both mediatlie[13] and immediately. Therefore seeing that it is God who is offended, only he is able to forgive.

Consider the incarnate Christ as he hung on the cross, craving God his Father for mercy towards his murderers, and saying, 'Forgive them Lord, they do not know what they are doing.' Yet when he himself forgave sins he thereby testified that he was truly God; thus the Church Fathers have taken this as clear evidence of his deity. When the kirk is said to forgive sins they only do so in the name and by the authority of Christ Jesus; in so doing they are announcing

---

[13] A sixteenth-century legal term referring to lands held and rights enjoyed, not directly of a superior but through a vassal; the sense therefore would appear to be of 'unwitting' sins compared to 'immediate' sins, that is, deliberate disobedience.

and proclaiming God's forgiveness, for as they speak his word they show themselves to be acting as his mouthpiece, and not speaking on their own initiative or instigation.

As to us who are brothers in Christ, we are charged to forgive others and we indeed do forgive them. But our action in forgiving them cannot replace God's forgiveness, for they are still guilty before him until he himself forgives them; he alone has the power to remove their guilt and wash away their sins. That is why David cries in Psalm 51:4, 'Against you, you only, have I sinned and done what is evil in your sight.' Therefore, since it is only God who can forgive sins, let us seek forgiveness from him and from him alone.

The cause that moves God to forgive sins

It still remains for us to enquire what it is that moves God to forgive a man's sins. Verse 17 tells us: 'In love you have delivered my life.' It was because God loved this man that he neither suffered the 'bitterness' ('Behold, it was for my welfare that I had great bitterness') to remain in his soul, nor his body to see the grave (*you* 'have delivered my life from the pit of destruction'). Hezekiah willingly admits that there was absolutely nothing in himself worthy of this love, and that therefore he was not deserving of God's love. Thus it stands to reason that his deliverance arose only on account of God's free love for him.

Read the Scriptures for yourselves. What is this that is done for us? Who is it who removes our sins, cancels our debt, so discharging us honourably and honestly? It is he who is both man and God, Christ Jesus. That is why the king quietly in these words acknowledges that his sins have been removed on account of God's love for him in Christ Jesus, who, though not yet born, was already within his loins according to the flesh. No other human being could ever have accomplished this, other than this man who is also God. For Christ is justly the only Mediator between God and man, and therefore whom the Lord God loves, he loves in him, and to whomsoever the Lord shows mercy, it is for his sake only. How can this be? Because he rendered perfect satisfaction for the entire wagon-load of all our sins as can be easily seen in three simple points.

First, he delivers us from our actual sins by giving full satisfaction on the cross as he suffered hell in his soul and death in his body, so delivering us from sin's penalty. Thus he is a perfect Mediator.

Second, he has delivered us from the cesspit and rotten root whence all our sins proceed. Christ Jesus was conceived in the womb of the Virgin through the mighty power of the Holy Spirit in order that our nature in him should be fully sanctified by the same Spirit. And this perfect purity of his human nature covers all our impurities. For he was not conceived in the corruption of sin as are we, but was entirely holy from the moment of his conception. So being himself completely pure, he was able to cover all our impurity.

Third, his perfection as our Mediator consists not only in the satisfaction he has rendered for all our sins, but also arises from his complete fulfilment of the whole law on our behalf. Actually, he accomplished the law far beyond any legal requirement in this way: the Second Table commands us to love our neighbours as ourselves, but he did more than that in that he died for us also. In his willing death, for he freely offered himself to God [Hebrews 9:14], he not only fulfilled the law for us, but went further than the law commanded.

This perfect righteousness of Christ comes between us and his Father, and covers our rebellion and disobedience, otherwise we could not be free from condemnation. In short, these three—perfect purity, perfect satisfaction, perfect righteousness—are to be found perfectly in Christ. Therefore all that remains for us is to seek from him mercy and forgiveness for all our sins. Whoever does not have Christ as his Intercessor shall never taste mercy.

Take note, therefore, of the application of this: What kind of intercession can Christ make for the one that blasphemes his Father? Surely, it is not possible that the Son can intercede for someone who wilfully and willingly blasphemes his Father. Of all judgments this must be most terrible when the spirit of blasphemy has such power to bring a man to utter such curses against his Maker.

The reason why the Lord forgave his sins

In verses 18 and 19, the king gives two reasons why the Lord forgave his sins. First, he shows that it was especially God's own glory that Hezekiah's life should be extended rather than be prematurely ended. Second, the king's deliverance from death would be a cause for praise down the generations and to the end of time: 'the father makes known to the children your faithfulness'; the result would be that believers in the future would turn to the Lord in their hour of need for like mercy. Thus for these two reasons, that God's glory would be seen both through the king's healing and throughout coming generations, the Lord bestowed restored health on his servant.

Let us consider more fully the first reason. 'For Sheol does not thank you; death does not praise you; those who go down to the pit do not hope for your faithfulness. The living, the living, he thanks you, as I do this day' (verses 18-19a). In other words he is saying, 'Dead men cannot praise you, not as we can who are still inhabiting our mortal bodies and are in your kirk. Those in their graves cannot look for the accomplishment of your promises, for if I was dead I could not expect you to fulfil your promise to me to give me a son. It is only the living, the living, who are able to praise you.' Notice how he repeats 'the living' to let us see that those who would praise the Lord aright must be endowed with a double life. So now the king says, 'Being restored to a double life, both in body and soul, I shall praise you, as only those who are alive as I am are able worthily to do.' That is the thrust of the first reason for God's mercy towards him.

However, we must be careful not to misunderstand what he means when he says that the dead do not praise the Lord: his meaning is that they no longer praise him in the same way as we do, that is, as living mortals here on earth. Indeed, there is no doubt that the souls of the departed saints are more ardent in their praise than when they were physically alive. How can this be? The nearer the soul is to God, the greater the pleasure and delight it has in him; to be absent from the body is to be present with the Lord. Greater pleasure in him can only mean greater praise to him, for there can be no pleasure in a saint's heart that does not return to God in praise. Where Christ has dwelt in someone during his earthly life, even though after death that believer's body turns to dust, yet the soul lives on in righteousness, for the Spirit of life raises that soul to heaven, just as that same Spirit that dwelt in Christ Jesus raised him up as a spiritual body. And as the Spirit of life enabled us to praise God in our earthly bodies, so even when we are absent from those bodies of clay, the same Spirit of life will likewise enable us to continue to praise him. It is as Paul says, 'But if Christ is in you, although the body is dead because of sin, the Spirit is life because of righteousness' (Romans 8:10). In other words, even when those who have departed from the 'land of the living' no longer praise God on earth, yet they never cease praising him.

The first of two observations

Two further observations regarding this. What is God's purpose in delivering out of any affliction a person, city or nation? His chief end of such deliverance is that that person, city or nation may serve as an instrument to proclaim his blessings, to sound his praise and to render heartfelt thanks for his salvation. If this is so, what nation or city that has been forgiven and delivered by God should then provoke him to anger by sliding back into even more grievous sins than before? Is this why God pardons us? Does he bestow his benefits upon us so that we can use them as weapons to fight against him? Is this not most certainly the highway to provoke him to even greater severity, and for him to sharpen the sword of his fury to use it against us? Indeed, what excuses can we offer when he deals with us harshly when it is we ourselves who have provoked him? There is no one in our nation who would not admit that we have been granted the most singular benefit ever when God delivered us from the terror of that nation which sought to conquer and subdue us; whoever refuses to acknowledge that must be a complete ass![14] Rightly weighed, considered and understood in the light of the Scriptures, this great deliverance stands historically second only to the mighty redemption of ancient Israel by the destruction of Pharaoh's army in the Red Sea.

But to what end did God deliver us? Is it that we should provoke him with even greater sins? Since the fear of our would-be conquerors has been banished, what sins are there with which our nation has not defiled herself? Is not even more blood shed among us, murder without mercy, oppression of the poor, law and justice trampled underfoot? In short, can you not see the chaos has increased to such an extent that the barons in our land act in their estates as if they are kings in their own right; what sort of monster shall be spawned among us by this chaos? There are only two alternatives. Either the Lord himself must intervene by causing our supreme magistrate, together with the local magistrates, firmly to stamp out this civil confusion, or else they themselves will be subjected by the barons to the same lawless treatment. It has to be one or the other. It cannot be both, for the thunderclouds of God's wrath are ready to break upon our nation. Our land is not able to bear this eruption of iniquity. As I have often said, if God has no means of punishing this wickedness among us, the very earth itself will be compelled to spew forth its inhabitants.

What is true of our nation in general is true of our capital city in particular, for even within this congregation there has never really been genuine, heart-felt thanks for God's mighty

---

[14] The reference is to the defeat of the Spaniard's 'Invincible Armada' in 1588.

deliverance from our foe. Already the Lord is letting us see that even though we have been preserved from foreigners descending upon us, nevertheless he can allow unexpected 'foreigners' to appear among us. For he has other means from within the very heart of our city with which to chastise us. Indeed, in the deeds of that braggard, at one time one of our neighbouring lords,[15] the Lord was beseeching us to reflect again on the greatness of his past benefits towards us; for if we will genuinely and gratefully acknowledge what he has done for our nation, there is no domestic threat that will cause us concern, as we saw in the outcome of that lord's scheming. It seemed to me that that man had sold himself to iniquity, as God's final judgment will make clear, unless the Lord, unknown to us, had mercifully intervened in his life with undeserved grace before he died—I most sincerely hope he did.

In the meantime, even though we rely on the Lord's great promises, constantly stand on guard lest by your failures and laxity God's glory and the freedom of our city be compromised in any way. So be watchful and alert so that as this city in the past has been a place of salutary warning to evil men, so it may continue to be to the likes of that braggard. For I have no doubt that when some trouble arises, it remains possible that the Lord's enemies could gain the upper hand. I digress in mentioning all this; yet it is my duty to uphold the good cause and to warn you also of your duty to be watchful.

---

[15] The reference is possibly to the treasonable attempts of the late Earl of Bothwell, who had been married to Mary Queen of Scots but who had died in 1578 in Dragsholm Castle in Denmark.

My second observation

The second observation I must make is that because God's glory is conjoined with the lives of his people, therefore as often as we advance his glory, we further our own salvation; if we neglect the one, we will also neglect the other. Seeing then that these two are inextricably bound together, for his sake let us all remember to set forth his glory in our lives inasmuch as we are able, each of us according to our station and vocation. Life here on earth can be difficult and sometimes very unhappy, and no one who sees the confusion in our nation rapidly increasing can expect an immediate redress of such trials. Thus with events here on earth so often miserable and confused, we would be constantly forlorn if we did not have the prospect of eternal joy in the hereafter.

The final verse of the psalm (verse 20)

'The Lord will save me, and we will play my music on stringed instruments all the days of our lives, at the house of the Lord.' Finally, the king declares that he will not only praise God for the present blessings he has received, but he also solemnly promises that so long as he lives he will never forget them, and will continue to bless God every day of his life. He will sing this song with his instrument in the Lord's house and before the congregation of his people because the blessings bestowed on him have been known to all. He will praise him in his body because his health had been restored, and he will praise him in his soul because he has been restored to his former spiritual joys. This is the import of the final verse.

This promise he makes clearly shows him to be full of gratitude. And if this good servant of God displays such thankfulness, how much more should we also be thankful since the Lord has delivered us in spite of our folly that had been about to cast us into such difficulties. For there was never a man who, as soon as Lord's heavy hand was lifted from him, did not then return to the dirt in which he had been wallowing like the sow that was washed, and to his former filth like dogs returning to their vomit.[16]

The conclusion

The chapter concludes by returning to the narrative. It has pleased the Holy Spirit to have the two final verses recorded for us and we should therefore be grateful for them. Since we have earlier considered the subject of the 'sign' for which Hezekiah asked, I shall not return to that. But we should notice the injunction given by Isaiah to the king to apply to the boil a poultice of dry figs that would bring healing. Hezekiah does as the prophet commanded.

We might be inclined to think that on this occasion Isaiah was taking on the role of a physician and laying aside his calling as a prophet. To some it might appear so. But we can be sure that he was only issuing instructions to the king that he himself had been told to give him. Therefore he continued in his prophetic office even when he gave the command to apply the poultice.

It remains for us to ask why the Lord did not choose to heal Hezekiah without commissioning the prophet to tell him to use a poultice. There were three reasons. First, to let the king see that ordinary medical means of healing (we might call them 'secondary causes') were not to be neglected or

---

[16] The allusion is to 2 Pet. 2:22.

condemned. Although God could heal perfectly well without such means, nonetheless he has given us various secondary causes, I mean medicaments, which are not to be despised. The second reason—and the most important one—was that the Lord knew that the king's faith was very weak; the prophet had assured him that in three days' time he would go into the temple,[17] yet the boil remained badly infected and his fever was still raging. The king must have wondered if the promise that he would be well enough to enter the temple very soon was possible; he could have scarcely believed it could come to pass. Therefore to support and strengthen his faith the Lord used the means of the fig poultice, for the more unexpected and unlikely the cure, the more our faith is awakened and stimulated. It is the same with the sacraments: water, bread and wine, simple things to be seen and handled, and all to strengthen our faith. And so the Lord gave the king a very simple cure to assure him that the promise of full healing within three days would be fulfilled.

The third reason was to teach Hezekiah that the Lord was the only true Physician of the body as well as of the soul. He controls and commands all remedies so that all cures take effect according to his will and good pleasure. Consequently, all illnesses also are under his command and control. Be assured of that. Therefore, unless God blesses the remedy applied, it will have no effect. What is true of medicaments is also true of those who till the soil; unless God blesses their toil and grants an increase, they will be disappointed and all their travail will be of no avail. So with physicians; even

[17] 2 Kings 20:5

though they instruct their patients to apply their various cures diligently, if the Lord chooses not to bless their work and withdraws his power from their secondary causes, the patient will know no improvement.

Thus the Lord gives a lesson to both the sick and the doctor. The patient must learn to look to God that the medicines being applied will have a good effect, even though they are only a means to an end. The doctor, for his part, must pray that the Lord will bless his work and that it may redound to God's glory and be used for the betterment of the patient. And where God is honoured and given first and last place, no doubt the means of healing will be blessed. Therefore, in all our troubles let everyone turn first of all to the Lord, and pray that he will be pleased to use the natural means he has provided,[18] and that he will bless both you and the cures used, all through his Son Christ Jesus. To whom be all praise, honour and glory, now and for ever. Amen.

[18] Bruce's phrase is, 'in God use his creatures': I assume that here Bruce is referring to herbs and various medicaments extracted or distilled from things God has created.

Appendix 1: On Conscience

The Preparation for the Lord's Supper[1]

But let a man examine himself, and so let him eat of that bread, and drink of that cup.—1 Corinthians 11:28

THE doctrine of our trial and due examination, well beloved in Christ Jesus, ought to come before the doctrine and receiving of the sacrament. No man can hear the word of God fruitfully without in some measure preparing his soul, and preparing the ear of his heart to hear, but preparation is always just as necessary for the receiving of the visible sacrament as for the hearing of the simple word. Therefore the doctrine of preparation and due examination should be given its proper place, and is very necessary for every one of you.

[1] Quoted by permission from *The Mystery of the Lord's Supper, Four Sermons Preached in St Giles, Edinburgh in 1589 by Master Robert Bruce,* translated and edited by T. F. Torrance. First published 1958 by James Clarke & Co., London. Second edition published by Christian Focus Publications, 2005, ISBN 978-1-84550-056-6.

In the words that we have read, the apostle offers his counsel and gives his advice, and not only his advice, but his admonition and command, that we should not come to the Table of the Lord, or come to the hearing of the word, rashly, but that every one of us should come to this holy action with reverence, that we should prepare and sanctify ourselves in some measure. Since we go to the Table of the King of heaven, it becomes us to put on our best apparel. In a word, he sets forth the whole doctrine and matter of such preparation when he says: 'Let every man and every woman try and examine themselves.'

It is as if he would say: 'Let every one of you try and examine your soul, that is, try the state of your own heart, and the condition of your own conscience. See what is the state of your heart with God, and what is the state of your conscience with your neighbour.' He does not ask your neighbour to try you; he does not ask your companion to try your heart; but he bids you personally to try your own conscience, and try your own heart, for no one can be certain of the state of your heart, or of the condition of your conscience, but you yourself.

Now, he does not exclude others from proving you, for it is the part of the pastor to try you, but no others can try you as strictly as you yourself can, for no man can know as much of you as you know of yourself. No one else can be certain of the state of your heart and the condition of your conscience, but you yourself may be certain of it. As for others, they may judge your heart and conscience according to your works and fruits, and unless your works and fruits are very wicked, and altogether vicious, we are bound in conscience to judge charitably of your heart and conscience. Thus no one is so fit to try the spirit of a man, to try the heart or conscience of a man, as the man himself.

If this trial is to be carried through well, three things have to be considered:—First, you have to understand what it is that you are to try; what you call a conscience, which the apostle commands you to try. Secondly, you have to weigh and consider the reasons and grounds why you should try your conscience. Thirdly, you have to see what the chief points are in which you should try and examine your conscience.

1. First, to begin with what is known to each of you, for there is none of you who lacks a conscience, it is necessary to understand what a conscience is. Therefore, as far as God gives me grace, I will explain it to you. I call a conscience a certain feeling in the heart, resembling the judgment of the living God, following upon a deed done by us, flowing from a knowledge in the mind, and accompanied by a certain motion of the heart, fear or joy, trembling or rejoicing.

Now let us examine the different parts of this definition. I call it first of all a certain feeling in the heart, for the Lord has left such a stamp in the heart of every man that he does not do anything so secretly or quietly without making his own heart strike him and smite him. God makes him feel in his own heart whether he has done well or ill. Why has the Lord placed this feeling in the heart? Because the eyes of God do not look so much upon the outward countenance and external behaviour, as upon the inward heart. For he says to Samuel in his first book (1 Samuel 16:7), 'The Lord beholds the heart.' Likewise in 1 Chronicles (28:9) he says to Solomon: 'The Lord searcheth all hearts, and understandeth all the imaginations of the thoughts.' Also Jeremiah says (11:20),

'The Lord tries the reins and the heart.' And the apostle in 1 Corinthians (4:5) says: 'The Lord will bring to light the hidden things of darkness, and make manifest the counsels of the hearts.' Therefore, because the Lord is concerned chiefly with the heart, it is in the heart that he places this feeling, which is the chief part of conscience.

Then I say that this feeling resembles the judgment of God, for this feeling was left and placed in our soul in order that we might have a domestic and familiar judgment within ourselves, to subscribe to and resemble the secret and invisible judgment of the high God—a particular judgment to go before that general judgment in that great day when every man shall be justified or damned, according to the particular judgment that is within his own conscience. In the meantime, this conscience is left in us as the means whereby the living God relates his acts in the last judgment to the whole process of our life on earth. For the books of our own conscience in that last day will be opened, and every man shall receive according to the report of the decree within his own conscience. Therefore, I say, our conscience resembles the judgment of God.

The third thing that I say is that it follows upon a deed done by us. Our conscience does not smite us before the deed is done, our heart does not strike us before the evil deed is committed. No, the stroke of the conscience and the feeling of the heart do not precede, but follow immediately upon the deed. Thus the deed is no sooner done, than your conscience applies it to yourself and gives out the sentence against you. Therefore, I say, it is a feeling following upon a deed done by us.

The fourth thing that I say is that it is a feeling flowing from a knowledge in the mind, for unless the conscience is informed and the heart knows that the thing which is done is evil, neither the heart nor the conscience can ever count it to be evil. Knowledge must go before the stroke of the conscience. Your heart can never feel that to be evil which your mind does not know to be evil. Therefore knowledge must ever go before feeling, and the testimony and stroke of your conscience will be in accordance with the measure of your knowledge. For a slight knowledge, a doubting and uncertain knowledge, makes the stroke of the conscience light and small, as on the other hand, a holy and solid knowledge drawn from the word of God, makes the stroke of the conscience heavy. Thus the conscience must answer to knowledge.

If we have no other knowledge but the knowledge which we have by nature, and by the spark of light still left in nature, our conscience will answer no further than to that knowledge. But if beside the light of nature we have a knowledge of God and his word, and a knowledge of God by his Holy Spirit working in our hearts, then our conscience will go further, excusing or accusing us, according to the light that is in the word. Thus the conscience is not acquired, or attained at the time we are enlightened by the working of the Holy Spirit and hearing of the word of God; but our conscience is born with us, is natural to us, and is left in the soul of every man and woman. As there are some sparks of light left in nature so there is a conscience left in it also. And if there were no more than that, that very light left in your nature would be enough to condemn you.

The conscience is not acquired, therefore, nor does it begin with the hearing of the word, or at the time when we begin to reform ourselves by the assistance and renewing of the Holy Spirit. Every man by nature has a conscience, and the Lord has left it in our nature. And even if this natural conscience is not reformed according to the word of God, it will be enough to condemn you eternally. Therefore, I speak of the feeling in the heart as flowing from a knowledge of the mind.

Last of all I say that it is accompanied with a certain motion of the heart; and we express this motion in fear or joy, trembling or rejoicing. It will be in very great fear if the deed is exceedingly heinous, and the stroke of the conscience is very heavy—then the conscience is never at rest, for guilt must always involve dread. But if the deed is honest, godly and commendable, it makes the heart glad, and even to break forth in joy. Thus, to be brief, in every conscience there must be two things: there must be a knowledge, and there must be a feeling whereby, according to your knowledge, you apply to your own heart the deed you have done. Thus, as the very word itself indicates, conscience consists of two parts: of knowledge, according to which it is called *science*, and of feeling, according to which the *con* is added—therefore *con-science*. The word *conscience* signifies, therefore, knowledge with application.

This conscience the Lord has appointed to serve in the soul of man for many uses, namely, to act as a keeper, a companion, a careful attendant on every action you do. Therefore, no action can be accomplished so secretly, so quietly, so surreptitiously, but that, whether you will or not, your conscience will bear testimony to it. Your conscience will be a faithful observer of it, and one day, a faithful recorder of that same action. And so

(1) the Lord has appointed your conscience to this office, that it may attend and wait upon you, in all your actions; nothing can escape it.

(2) Likewise, the Lord has appointed your conscience, and placed it in your soul, to be your accuser, so that when you do any evil deed, you have a private accuser within your own soul, to find fault with it. And

(3) He has also placed it within your soul to be a true and steadfast witness against you. Yes, the testimony of the conscience not only resembles a testimony or a witness, but the conscience is as good as ten thousand witnesses.

(4) The conscience is also left in your soul to act the part of a judge against you, to declare the sentence against you, to condemn you. And so it does, for our particular judgment must precede the general and universal judgment of the Lord at that great day. And what more?

(5) He has left your conscience within you to put your own sentence into execution against yourself. This is terrible. He has left it within you to be a torment and a scourge to yourself, and so to put your own sentence into execution.

Is not this something more than wonderful, that one and the self-same conscience should serve so many ends in a soul, as to be a continual observer and marker of your actions, an accuser, ten thousand witnesses, a judge, an executioner and tormentor, to execute your own sentence against yourself? Thus the Lord never needs to seek a member of court outside of your own soul in order to conduct a lawful process against you, for you have all these within yourself. Take note of this, for there is not a word of this that shall fall to the ground, but you will find it either to your weal, or to your everlasting woe.

This secret and particular judgment that every one of you carries about with you, remains so surely and firmly embedded within you, that do what you can to blot it out, you will never get it eradicated from your soul. If you were to become as malicious and as wicked as ever any incarnate devil upon the earth, you would never get this conscience altogether eradicated from your soul; but, whether you will or not, there would always remain sufficient of it to make you inexcusable in the great day of the general judgment.

I grant that you may blot out all knowledge from your mind, and make yourself as blind as a mole; I grant also that you may harden your heart so as to blot out all feeling from it, so that your conscience will not accuse you, or find fault with you, and you will even have a delight in doing evil without any remorse, but I deny that any degree of wickedness on the earth will bring you to the point where you may do evil without fear. The more you do evil, the longer you continue in evil-doing, the greater will be your fear. Yes, in spite of the devil, and in spite of all the malice of the heart of man, that fear will remain. And even if they should both conspire together, it would not be in their power to banish that fear, for the gnawing of the conscience will ever remain to testify to you that there is a day of judgment.

I grant also that conditions will change from time to time, that fear will not always remain, but will sometimes give way to security. Neither will that security always remain, but will give way again to fear, so that it will not be possible to get this fear wholly eradicated. The greater the security is, the greater will your fear be when you are awakened.

I grant, again, that this fear will be blind, for from the time a man by evil-doing has banished knowledge from his mind, and feeling from his heart, what can there remain, but a blind fear? When men have put out all light and left nothing in their nature but darkness, there can remain nothing but a blind fear. So I grant that fear is blind, for neither do they know where fear comes from, what progress it makes, and where it leads to, nor do they know where and when it will end. Therefore those who are in this way misguided in their souls are of all men on earth the most miserable. As long as you keep in your mind a spark of this knowledge and spiritual light, by which you may see the face of God in Christ, by which you may see an escape in the death and passion of Christ, and by which you may see God's compassionate mercy offered in the blood of Christ, if you have any spark of this light, even if it be ever so little, to direct you, and even if this knowledge were very severely damaged, yet there is mercy enough for you in Christ. But if you close up all the windows of your soul and your heart, and fill them with palpable darkness, so that you neither know where the terror comes from, nor see any way of escaping it, that is the misery of all miseries.

We have much to lament; we have the state of this country to lament, for they are not present to whom this preaching specially applies. Even so, there is not one of you who should not now take heed to your conscience, while leisure is given to you, in order that you may not banish altogether this light which is still offered to you, some sparks of which still remain. I see most of our great men in this country running headlong to extinguish the spark of light that is in them, and they will not rest until it is utterly extinguished. And when they have done so, what can follow, alas, but a blind and terrible fear in their conscience which they can never have eradicated, a fear without a way of escape, a fear that grows and does not decay, a fear that will devour them wholly at the last?

Therefore let every one of you take heed to this light that is within you, take heed that the foul affections of your heart do not draw your bodies after them; see at least that these affections do not banish this light. And so long as the Lord offers you this light in time, pray that in his mercy he may give you the grace to embrace it, to enter a new course, and to amend your lives while you still have time.

The body will leave the soul, and the soul will leave the body, but the conscience will never leave the soul. But wherever the soul goes, to the same place will the conscience repair, and in whatever state your conscience is, when you die, in the same state it will meet you on that great day. Therefore if your conscience is a torment to you at the time of your death, if you do not get it pacified then, it will be your executioner at the final judgment.

Therefore this matter must be well considered, and every one of you should endeavour to have a good conscience, that when the soul is severed from the body, leaving your conscience at rest and peace with God, it may be restored to you, and meet you again with as great peace and quietness. So much, then, for the conscience, and what it is. I pray that the living God may so sanctify your memories that you may keep these things, and that every one of them may remain with you in such a way that to the end of your life you may remember them.

2. The second thing we have to speak of is this: we must try to consider why we should examine our conscience. What are the reasons that should move men or women to try their own consciences and souls? I shall answer briefly.

(1) It becomes every one of you to try your conscience because the Lord makes his residence in it, and in no other part of the soul. He has appointed his dwelling to be in the heart of man, in his will and conscience, and therefore it becomes you to make his dwelling-place clean, and to take heed to your heart.

(2) Even if the Lord of heaven were not to make his residence there, nevertheless the eye of God is all-seeing, able to pierce through the thickness of man's flesh, however dark and gross it may be, and to pierce right through into the secret corners of your conscience. To the all-seeing eye of God, the most secret corner of your conscience is as open, clear and manifest as any outward or bodily thing on earth can be to the outward eye of the body. Therefore because his eye is so piercing and because he casts his eye only upon our heart, it becomes us to try our hearts.

(3) He is the Lord of the conscience. No earthly monarch has any sovereignty or lordship over the conscience. Only the God of heaven, only Christ Jesus, King of heaven and earth, is Lord of the conscience. He only has power to save and loose. Therefore when you prepare to come to the Lord's Table, is it not fitting that you should look at your conscience, try and examine its state?

(4) One of the chief reasons why it becomes you to try and examine your conscience is because the health and welfare of your soul depend upon it. If your conscience within your soul is well, if it is at peace and rest, your soul is well. If your conscience is in a good state, your soul must be in a good state. If your conscience is in good health, your soul must necessarily be in good health, for the good health and weal of your soul depend upon a good conscience. Therefore it becomes every one of you to try your conscience well. No law was ever set down or devised that made it unlawful for us to take care of ourselves. It is lawful for us to seek the things that procure, preserve and maintain our health.

Now, since the health of your soul consists in the health of your conscience, and in preserving it, therefore in accordance with all law, you ought to attend to your conscience. If you keep your conscience well, your soul is in health, and if your soul is in health, no matter what troubles may come upon your body, you will endure them all. But if your soul is diseased, and if that pining sickness brought on by an evil conscience lays hold upon your soul, you will not be able to endure the smallest trouble that can come upon your body; whereas if the conscience is at rest and in good health, no trouble can come upon your body but the strength of a good conscience will be more than a match for it. Have you not reason, therefore, and more than reason, to take heed to your conscience, to examine and to try its state and disposition?

Now, because it is a savourless jest to tell you that health is necessary, and not to show you how that health may be acquired, preserved, and maintained, therefore to keep your conscience in quietness and in good health, I shall give you these few lessons. First of all, take care to keep a steadfast persuasion of the mercy of God in Christ Jesus. When you lie down, and when you rise up, examine your relation with God, and see whether you may look for mercy at his hand or not.

Are you persuaded of his mercy? Be assured, then, that your conscience is in a good condition, that you have health in your soul; for by the keeping of faith, the conscience is preserved, as the apostle says in 1 Timothy 1:19. Keep this persuasion, preserve it whole and sound; do not hurt it; try not to let your soul into doubt; do not let anything hinder your persuasion, if you would keep your soul in health. If you doubt or in any way weaken your persuasion and assurance, then assuredly there will follow at the same time loss of health in your soul. It is inevitable, too, that your conscience will be hurt at the same time, and faith will not dwell except in a healthy conscience. Therefore whenever you do anything against your conscience, you immediately weaken your persuasion of the mercy of God, and you will continue to doubt his mercy and want health in your conscience until you fall down at the feet of Christ, obtain mercy for that evil deed, gain peace at his hand, and repair your persuasion. This then is the first lesson: in order to preserve your souls in health, be sure that you are persuaded of God's mercy.

The second lesson is that you must flee, eschew and forsake whatever may trouble the health of your soul....

The third lesson is this: study to do well. If you want to keep health in your soul, study to do better and better continually, at least have a purpose in your heart to do better daily. That is the last lesson. ...

Appendix 2: Additional Sermon

An Exhortation to the Presbyteries of Lothian
by Master Robert Bruce,
Minister of Christ's Evangel at Edinburgh,
16th September, 1589

Study to show thyself approved unto God, a workman that
needs not be ashamed, dividing the word of truth aright.
—2 Timothy 2:15

IT is not unknown, brothers, that in Timothy we have set down the true pattern of a profitable pastor: how he should behave himself in all things, what he should do, what he should leave undone, what he should follow, what he should flee. In everything he is forewarned but chiefly, among many, of one thing, that he study not to please men: that he hunt not for their praise and commendation.

For why? Experience from time to time has taught that such men have not only imperilled their own estate, but hazarded also the whole estate of the kirk. There were two in the days of Timothy who, to get a name among men that they were curious disputers and subtle reasoners, moved doubts upon everything, chopping and changing the truth of God as if it had been the profane word of mere mortal man. Ultimately, they began to ask questions and to raise doubts upon the very articles of our belief.

The spirit of the devil so carried them forward that doubting finally came to plain defection. They denied the resurrection in particular. So, they not only lost themselves and poisoned their hearers, but they perverted the truth of God so far as in them lay. From these men's example, the apostle warned Timothy, and through him every pastor, to be aware not only of this vain jangling about words, especially in matters of conscience, but chiefly to be aware of the root and fountain wherefrom they spring—that natural self-love which we all nourish in our bosoms, and are so loath to part with all our days.

We have an example in our time of a man going about to make himself great and to get the praise of men, who in the end not only hazarded his own estate but imperilled the estate of the whole kirk, so far as lay in him.[1] So, as the example of Hymenaeus was used to alert Timothy to be aware of such a vice, so let the example of our Hymenaeus, who is still fresh in our memories, alert us that we fall not into the same snare. Let it warn us not only not to hunt for the praise of men, but also that we resolve to turn from the root and fountain from which it springs—that natural self-love which every one of us has a portion. Since we are enrolled into the school of Christ, let us study to learn this one lesson, to renounce ourselves.

[1] Bruce is referring to Patrick Adamson, the late Bishop of St Andrews.

The Lord give us hearts to learn it, and make us both to be born again and to renounce ourselves in this life. This is not the work of man but the singular work of God renewing man!

Now as he has shown him what he must avoid and the vice from which he should chiefly flee, so in this verse, he begins to admonish him that its opposite is the chief virtue which he should embrace, and the only target he should shoot at during his whole life, that is, to 'study to be approved of God'. For seeing there is no workman who does not long to be praised for his work (it is a common instinct in us all to seek to be approved), the apostle informs and admonishes Timothy what sort of approval he must seek, at whose hands he shall seek it, and in what way he shall gain it.

I. The kind of approval pastors should seek

The sort of approbation we are to seek must be spiritual and godly, flowing from the Spirit of God and not from flesh and blood. As it must flow from the Spirit of God, so we must seek it only at the hands of God and not of any other. We must study to be approved of him.

God's approval

Why? Suppose men approve you, you are not then more approved. For if you, in the absence of praise from others, should praise yourself, you are never a hair the better. 'If a man honour himself, his honour is worth nothing' (John 8). And he whom men commend 'is not approved' (2 Cor. 10:12), but only he who is commended by God. Therefore, let us not seek honour one from another, but let us seek the honour that comes from God only and to be approved of him.

Man's approval

When we get God's approbation, we shall get two other commendations. If God approves us, he shall make our own conscience approve us. And if our own conscience and God within our conscience approve us, we have two of the best. For these two will never leave us; they will stand by us here on earth. Then when we come before a higher tribunal they will make us blithe.

The kirk's approval

As to the third sort of approval which is by men, where these two go before, we shall get the kirk of God (no doubt) and good men to approve us. For where God and conscience call a man inwardly, God makes his kirk ratify his calling outwardly, as we see he commands the kirk to separate Paul and Barnabas to the work to which he called them inwardly. So, when we get his approbation we shall get all three.

Therefore, let us look for no other approval but his. We look to his approbation when we look to himself. He honours us when we honour him. When we seek nothing but him, then he seeks us and our good. It is far better for us that he seek our good than that we ourselves seek it, for he seeks it best. Therefore let us seek God and his honour, and leave our honour entirely to him. When we consider who has sent us forth, who employs us, who made us Christ's ambassadors, we will conclude that we ought to study to please none but him. We shall render account to none but him.

II. The pastor and his work

The apostle shows us we must do two things to win divine approval. First, we must study to have a solicitous care to present ourselves to him: second, that we study to present our work of ministry to him; as Paul says, 'Study to show yourself approved to God' and again, '… a workman who does not need to be ashamed'. So we are to be both good Christians and good pastors.

The pastor's own life

There is no standing before God but in purity of heart, for it is the pure heart that looks upon God and stands before him. The heart is only purged by faith. So it is by faith alone that we stand and present ourselves to God. To be approved, the good pastor must study to increase both faith and sanctification. For he shall never teach with authority and power except he knows in himself what he longs to work in others. How shall he press to sanctify others who is not sanctified himself? How shall he teach holily who is not holy? So we must study to our own personal sanctification to ensure as we teach salvation to others we are not reprobates ourselves.

The pastor's work

We must also study to present our works and how we have travailed before him. That is, we must study to show ourselves good pastors as well as good Christians. To this effect he lets us see what qualities are required of us to do the work of a pastor. First of all, he shows us that we must not be idle, for the ministry is work and not idleness. Because men may work with a wrong attitude and in the wrong way, he exhorts we must be workmen 'who need not be ashamed', that is, work-men without reproof.

There is a third thing: the pastor must be a skilful work-man that can cut and work rightly. At the end of the verse he shows whereupon he shall work and wherein he shall toil and that is upon the word of truth. Because none of this can be done without great labour, he bids him study them all.

To come back to the point that we must be workmen and not idlers, the apostle says in 1 Thess. 5:12, 'I pray you to acknowledge these that labour among you and have them in great estimation for their work's sake.' So the ministry is a work, and we are workmen.

III. Ruling and teaching

The work of ministry stands in two points: ruling and teach-ing. For ruling, we have 1 Thess. 5:12, '... and rule you in the Lord'. For teaching, 1 Tim. 5:17 lets us see that they must 'labour in the word'. Because it is possible to work in the wrong attitude of mind and even to labour diligently but in the wrong way, he enjoins that we be such workmen 'as need not be ashamed', that is, worthy workmen without reproof. For the ministry is a worthy work (1 Tim. 3:1).

Ruling as Christ ruled

Ruling rightly means ruling 'in the Lord'. That means to rule spiritually in spiritual affairs as the Lord himself did. To rule 'in the Lord' does not mean to rule as a lord, for 'we preach Jesus Christ as Lord and ourselves your servants for his sake'. We therefore rule under the Lord as servants, as he was a servant. He came not to do his own will, but his Father's will who sent him. As the Lord ruled not after his own will, far less must we rule after our wills. We must lay aside our wills and follow the will of God only. Many determinations flow from men's wills, but they must be laid aside. Even the will of the monarch outwith the warrant of God's word can have no more power to strike the conscience than the Pope's edicts. God's will is perfect and good and holy (Rom. 12:2).

Further, to rule as the Lord ruled, the pastor must rule carefully and diligently. The Lord said it was his food and drink to do the Father's will. So we must be careful to prefer his work over any work of our own, even though it may concern the most intimate matters pertaining to ourselves.

To move us to diligence, we should remember that we have the city of God to watch over; we have the spouse of Christ to present as a pure virgin; we have the lambs of Christ committed to our feeding. In that threefold repetition of our Master, bidding Peter feed his lambs, what was required but diligence? Who is able to answer to the meanest of these things? And yet I have not spoken of half of the things that are requisite.

On the one hand, I marvel there are many loath to put their shoulders under so heavy a burden. Yet on the other hand, it remains a great marvel that any should be found that can take upon themselves so weighty and difficult a work. So much so, whoever may aspire to this task unsent will never do any good in his work.

Teaching skilfully

As the pastor must rule rightly so he must teach skilfully. The apostle bids pastors divide the word, and divide it aright. The form of words he uses I take to be borrowed and alludes to the family's bread, comparing the word to household bread and us to stewards who are dividers of that bread. As it is required in any steward of a great family that he be discreet in such a way that he has respect to each person's age, ability and needs so as to apportion to them accordingly, so in us who are dispensers of this blessed word there is a special kind of dexterity needed, that is, a gift of discretion whereby we may skilfully and fruitfully divide the word to each one.

Whoever would act as a skilful teacher must be a faithful interpreter and a skilful applier. He must take care to attend to three things before anything else. First, to ascertain and understand as near as possible the true meaning of the writer. In order to do this he must first study what the words signify; he must test their meaning and then gather the interpretation the words will carry. For if he reaches a wrong understanding of the words of Scripture, or attributes to them some other meaning they do not have, he becomes a perverter of the word.

Second, in order to see if the meaning he has arrived at is right, he must compare his text with other parts and places of Scripture, to see how it agrees with the ongoing message of God. If he finds his interpretation harmonises, most likely he has the true sense.

The third thing he must do is to note how the words of his text are placed and in what order they come and how they relate to the context—what has gone before and what follows.

Sufficiency of Scripture

But he that would interpret truly must chiefly take heed to the Scriptures, for all true interpretations must be sought out of the Scriptures. Seeing that all truth is contained in the Scriptures, there can be no true interpretation but that which flows from them. Men should never turn to their own inventions if they cannot find what they want in the Scriptures. For no man should use a lie to interpret a truth; for the words of men, without Scripture, are only lies and vanities.

Also if the interpreter would have sensitivity (as he ought and should), of force he must use Scriptures. He must compare one place with another place, for some truth which he finds obscurely spoken in one place he will find it more clearly spoken in another. Therefore many scriptures are necessary, and he that would interpret truly, must have many scriptures in his memory. Therefore we should pray for holy memories, for our old memories will not keep these things: they must be sanctified memories that will keep holy things.

Applying Scripture

As he must be a faithful interpreter, so he must be a skilful applier, for he must 'divide the word aright'. It is not enough simply to apply unless he apply skilfully. So skilful application is necessary. It is not possible to feed upon food, except it be applied to our mouths. Likewise, it is not possible that our souls can feed except spiritual food be applied. If the food be applied to any other part but the mouth the application serves nothing; likewise in spiritual things. If they be not applied to the right parts, and to the right diseases, the application may do them more harm than good. Therefore, it is necessary that he who would do the part of a skilful applier know the faults and diseases of his flock, which is not possible in this town, except it were divided into parishes that every one might have a reasonable number that look to him and he were acquainted with and accustomed to their manners and behaviour.

Thus application is a chief point of the pastor's office, for there is no edifying beside it; there is no obedience to God without it; and, therefore as by interpretation he informs the mind, and makes it understand what should or should not be done, so by application he should subdue the will, that it may give obedience and follow the understanding.

Candidates for the ministry

Then in a word, we see that the gifts of government and of exhortation are necessarily requisite to be in a pastor in some measure. Indeed no one can be a pastor except he have at least something of both these gifts. Therefore you must take heed to your admission. In admitting young men, you should see how they have profited in both these gifts; and that act passed in the last Assembly should be taken seriously, and none be placed in this office except he have drunken in by time the gift of government, together with the gift of teaching, in some measure.

And as for application, it is so necessary if it were no more but to turn over the very words of the text upon the hearer, it must not be omitted. Indeed, the nearer that we go to God's word, the application is so much the better, for his word must aye have a greater force with it than any other word. And when the people hear that it is God speaking and not man, it strikes a great reverence in their hearts. So much the more when we consider the worthiness and dignity of the subject on which we ought to take these pains and entreat men.

Reverence, humility and painful travail

The apostle calls it here 'the word of truth'. The more notable any subject is, the more wisely should it be handled. We have not such a notable subject as this, for there is not a subject that has these epithets, to be called sound, healthsome, holy, and true but this. Indeed, beside this there is neither health, soundness, truth, nor holiness. Therefore we should not chop nor change the word, as if it were a vain word. Rather with great reverence and humility it should be handled.

Who is able to do these things or to answer to the meanest part of them? These things demand accuracy and diligence, singular care and painful travail. They are not gained by sluggishness; nor will they allow us to be employed in other matters. Rather they demand the whole man and that the ministry of the word be the one great thing in which he engage. That is why the apostle uses the word 'study', showing that these things are not come by without study, that is, without solicitous care and utmost diligence.

Praying in the Spirit

All this can be summed up in two words: ourselves and our office. If we study in faith and in a good conscience, there is no doubt but that we shall take heed to ourselves and to our calling. But these two we cannot keep unless we study also a third, I mean the One who guards all these treasures, namely, the Holy Spirit. We must study to entertain and cultivate Him. This will be done mainly by praying in the Holy Spirit. Therefore, we should be acquainted with prayer, and be instant in it, that the Lord will not withdraw his Spirit from us but rather increase his power in us day by day, that we may find by experience and by a genuine assurance, the truth of his heavenly promises within ourselves, especially that promise of everlasting life. It is to this life that Christ Jesus, the great Pastor of the sheep, who gave his life for the flock, will bring us! To him, with the Father and the Holy Spirit be all honour, praise and glory for ever. Amen.

Other titles in the Puritan Paperback Series
published by the Banner of Truth Trust

The Acceptable Sacrifice, John Bunyan

All Loves Excelling, John Bunyan

All Things for Good, Thomas Watson

Apostasy from the Gospel, John Owen

The Art of Prophesying, William Perkins

The Bruised Reed, Richard Sibbes

Christ Set Forth, Thomas Goodwin

Christian Love, Hugh Binning

The Christian's Great Interest, William Guthrie

Come and Welcome to Jesus Christ, John Bunyan

Communion with God, John Owen

The Crook in the Lot, Thomas Boston

The Lord's Supper, Thomas Watson

The Love of Christ, Richard Sibbes

The Mortification of Sin, John Owen

The Mystery of Providence, John Flavel

Prayer, John Bunyan

Precious Remedies Against Satan's Devices, Thomas Brooks

The Rare Jewel of Christian Contentment, Jeremiah Burroughs

The Reformed Pastor, Richard Baxter

The Secret Key to Heaven, Thomas Brooks

Sermons of the Great Ejection

The Shorter Catechism, Thomas Vincent

The Sinfulness of Sin, Ralph Venning

Smooth Stones from Ancient Brooks, Thomas Brooks

The Spirit and the Church, John Owen

Spiritual-Mindedness, John Owen

A Sure Guide to Heaven, Joseph Alleine

Temptation: Resisted & Repulsed, John Owen

The True Bounds of Christian Freedom, Samuel Bolton

The Banner of Truth Trust originated in 1957 in London. The founders believed that much of the best literature of historic Christianity had been allowed to fall into oblivion and that, under God, its recovery could well lead not only to a strengthening of the church, but to true revival.

Inter-denominational in vision, this publishing work is now international, and our lists include a number of contemporary authors as well as classics from the past. The translation of these books into many languages is encouraged.

A monthly magazine, *The Banner of Truth,* is also published. More information about this and all our publications can be found on our website or supplied by either of the offices below.

THE BANNER OF TRUTH TRUST

3 Murrayfield Road
Edinburgh, EH12 6EL
UK

PO Box 621, Carlisle
Pennsylvania, 17013
USA

www.banneroftruth.org